DEWEY ON EDUCATION

Appraisals

STUDIES IN EDUCATION

DEWEY

ON

EDUCATION

Appraisals

Edited with an Introduction by

Reginald D. Archambault

BROWN UNIVERSITY

RANDOM HOUSE
NEW YORK

ACKNOWLEDGMENTS

I am grateful to the following for permission to reprint from works on which they hold the copyright:

Cambridge University Press for selections from *Truth and Fallacy in Educational Theory*, by Charles D. Hardie, 1942.

Harper and Row for selections from *John Dewey's Challenge to Education*, by Oscar Handlin, 1959, and *Education Between Two Worlds*, by Alexander Meiklejohn, 1942.

The *Harvard Educational Review* for "Educational Liberalism and Dewey's Philosophy," by Israel Scheffler, Vol. XXVI, No. 2, Spring, 1956, pp. 190–198, and "The Philosophical Bases of the Experience Curriculum," by Reginald D. Archambault, Vol. XXVI, No. 3, Summer, 1956, pp. 263–375. Professor Scheffler also kindly consented to permit the reprinting of his article.

Little, Brown and Co., The Atlantic Monthly Press for selections from *Quackery in the Public Schools*, by Albert Lynd, 1953.

The New Leader and Sidney Hook for "John Dewey: His Philosophy of Education and Its Critics," a supplement to *The New Leader*, Vol. XLII, No. 1, November 2, 1959.

Phi Delta Kappan for "John Dewey's War on Dualism," by Philip H. Phenix, Vol. XLI, October 1959, pp. 5–9.

The Philosophy of Education Society for "The Vain Quest for Unity," by Frederic Lilge, reprinted from the *Proceedings of the Fifteenth Annual Meeting*, 1959.

The Saturday Review and Jerome Bruner for "After John Dewey, What?," Vol. XLIV, June 17, 1961, pp. 58–59, 76–78.

School and Society for "John Dewey and Progressive Education Today," by M. I. Berger, Vol. LXXXVII, March 28,

1959, pp. 140–142, and for "Personal Reminiscences of Dewey and My Judgment of His Present Influence," by William Heard Kilpatrick, Vol. LXXXVII, October 10, 1959, pp. 374–375.

The University of Chicago Press for "John Dewey and the Progressive-Education Movement," by Lawrence A. Cremin, reprinted from the *School Review*, Vol. LXVII, Summer, 1959, pp. 160–173.

CONTENTS

Philosophy and Education

Progressive Education

In Prospect

INTRODUCTION

This book represents an attempt to provide a balanced selection of critical appraisals of John Dewey's philosophy of education. In recent years and particularly during 1959, the centenary of Dewey's birth, a number of evaluations of his work were published, many of which were collected in books or in special issues of journals. But because of the nature of the occasion most of these selections tended to be eulogistic. Critical pieces published at other times have usually fallen into two categories: those that are "apologies" written by followers anxious to defend Dewey against all real or imagined attacks; and the indictment by those who, for whatever motive, are anxious to decry Dewey's "aesthetic materialism," his "shirt-tail pragmatism," his "country-club existentialism," his "easy philosophy of life adjustment." Most of the collected volumes of appraisals of Dewey's work are highly laudatory, consisting of appreciations rather than critical analyses of his central philosophical ideas. Responsible pieces of criticism are difficult to come by, because they are scattered throughout journals and books and because there are really so few of them.

This paucity of sophisticated criticism of Dewey is interesting in itself. One must speculate on the reasons, but the primary one is probably that there are very few philosophical critics who have turned serious attention to Dewey's educational theory. Philosophers, in their evaluations, have concentrated most heavily on his basic philosophy in their reluctance to deal with the more practical aspects of his theory. This is unfortu-

nate and ironic, for Dewey himself has said in an autobiographical essay:

> ... Although a book called *Democracy and Education* was
> for many years that in which my philosophy, such as it
> is, was most fully expounded, I do not know that philo-
> sophic critics, as distinct from teachers, have ever had
> recourse to it. I have wondered whether such facts sig-
> nified that philosophers in general, although they are
> themselves usually teachers, have not taken education with
> sufficient seriousness for it to occur to them that any
> rational person could actually think it possible that phi-
> losophizing should focus about education as the supreme
> human interest in which, moreover, other problems, cos-
> mological, moral, logical, come to a head. At all events,
> this handle is offered to any subsequent critic who may
> wish to lay hold of it.[1]

A major reason for publishing this volume is to bring
together analyses of Dewey's basic philosophical
thought as it relates to the central problems of education.

The volume itself has a loose form of organization,
divided as it is into six major sections. The prefatory
section, consisting of a reminiscence and appreciation
by William Heard Kilpatrick, is an appropriate introduction to the volume, for it reflects Dewey's influence
on educational theorists in general, and the "Columbia
School" in particular. It is also representative of the
depth of admiration and appreciation which many of
his followers hold for him.

Two selections are included to provide historical
prospective. Lawrence Cremin's piece assays the development of the Progressive Education movement,
broadly perceived, and Dewey's role in it. It is an excellent example of the type of scholarship that criticism
of Dewey often lacks, for Cremin makes a true effort

[1] John Dewey, "From Absolutism to Experimentalism," in G. P.
Adams and W. P. Montague, eds., *Contemporary American Philosophy* (New York: Macmillan, 1930), pp. 22 f.

to examine Dewey's actual statements and intentions rather than the distorted versions that are often offered by others. The subtlety of the philosopher's views is emphasized, and the tendency to distort and over-simplify them is not only avoided but criticized. Cremin demonstrates that Dewey was at once a proponent and a critic of "Progressive" education.

Oscar Handlin is also concerned with the historical setting of Dewey's views. He uses the formative years as a focal point and describes the social conditions that generated Dewey's truly creative approach to education, and in doing so provides us with a rich bibliography of writings by and about Dewey during the early period. Cremin makes a strong case for distinguishing "Dewey as observer" from "Dewey as reformer," and Handlin's essay lends support to the view that a complete understanding of him can be gained only after examining the conditions against which he reacted. For Dewey, true to his pragmatic bias, did indeed use philosophy as a means for solving pressing social problems, the most important of which he found in the educational situation. However, his solutions were not merely immediate, for, dealing as they did with generalizable problems, they were central and hence relevant to a wide range of specific issues. Handlin notes this in his evaluation of the contemporary relevance of Dewey's early critique.

The third section consists of two essays that deal with Dewey's treatment of what was for him the central focal point in all of his thinking: the quest for unity in a world of diverse and antagonistic elements. He saw the tendency to employ dualism as the greatest detriment to progress in philosophy, splitting categories artificially, and culminating in the divorce, in educational theory, of liberal and professional, subject matter and method, psychological and logical thinking, discipline and freedom. Philip Phenix explores Dewey's central attack on dualism and then proceeds to relate it to five important contemporary issues in order to demonstrate the persistent relevance of his views. Phenix finds that the tendency to consider problems in terms of polarities is still prevalent and suggests that the Deweyan view of the unity of apparent opposites could help in the solution of many of these issues.

Frederic Lilge is also concerned with Dewey's quest for unity but concentrates on the political sphere. Traditional political theory dealt with the dilemma of unity and diversity and the need for reconciling the conflict between the individual on one hand and the society on the other. Dewey considered education to be both individual and social. Subject matter represented the content of social life, method the capacities of the child in dealing with that content. Habits, which serve as the basis for individual conduct, are social in origin. Maximum individuality, combined with responsible social participation, would result from an educational system that blended the needs of the individual and the demands of the social group. The scientific-democratic method was to serve as the chief means for effecting this result. In a highly ambitious essay, Lilge considers the various manifestations of this view. Dewey's treatment of social means, idealized social ends, instrumentalities and consummatory ends are examined in critical detail, and Lilge concludes that Dewey failed to reconcile these tensions in his philosophy, or provided only a superficial reconciliation that de-emphasizes individualism, and therefore left us with an inadequate and irrelevant philosophy.

The next section is made up of five essays that deal with more technical philosophical considerations as they relate to education. Alexander Meiklejohn writes with deep appreciation and fervid criticism of Dewey's view of the basic relation between knowledge and intelligence and in so doing considers a wide range of specific issues and their educational implications. He claims that Dewey's view of the relations between theory and practice, knowledge and intelligence, facts and values, knowledge and wisdom, is deep in ambiguity. This ambiguity is due in great part, he says, to the tendency toward superficial unity of distinct aspects that is noted by Lilge. Here, it is the unsuccessful merging of the objective, the scientific, the evidential, the verifiable, with the subjective, habitual, instinctive, and the emotive that serves as a center of attention. Meiklejohn maintains that the ambiguous relation between these two aspects of action leads Dewey to two modes of interpretation stemming from a temporary emphasis on one or the other pole: the "objective" and the "subjective" Dewey. The result, Meiklejohn claims, is a theory which generates confusion, one which is intrinsically conducive to the various kinds of interpretation and misinterpretation which actually befell it in the hands of his many followers in educational theory. The problem dealt with here is actually the classic one of the relation between desire and desirability, but Meiklejohn, taking his cue from Dewey, properly discusses that issue and its implications in the context of the educational problem.

Israel Scheffler, too, sees Dewey's tendency to merge concepts traditionally kept distinct as something of a mixed blessing, helpful because it breaks down artificial and superficial categories, but detrimental in its effective elimination of proper distinctions. Scheffler offers two examples of this failure in Dewey's writing. The first, the failure to adequately distinguish the realms of theory and practice, opens the way to a form of subtle anti-intellectualism in Dewey's antagonism to "pure theory" divorced from action. The second example is Dewey's failure to distinguish between problem-solving as a methodological device and problem-solving as a basis for content selection. These criticisms strike at the heart of Dewey's theory, for they confront two central notions in his philosophy of education: the pragmatic theory of meaning and the continuity of subject matter and method.

C. D. Hardie's essay was written much earlier than the others which appear in this volume. It is part of an extremely influential book, *Truth and Fallacy in Educational Theory*, published in 1942. The book is important because it represents an early attempt to apply techniques of linguistic analysis to problems in educational theory. His is a frontal attack on pragmatism in general, and its theory of truth in particular. Hardie focuses on the problematic context employed by pragmatists. Then, in a fashion exemplary of the way in which basic philosophical issues can be legitimately related to problems in education, he draws out the implications of this discussion for a theory of curriculum and method. His analysis is wide-ranging, dealing not only with Dewey's instrumental logic, but with his theory of valuation and his view of experimental method as well.

Sidney Hook's essay is a long, incisive, and wide-ranging defense of Dewey's educational theory by one of his most learned, objective, and sophisticated followers. He discusses every phase of Dewey's philosophy of education, but does so in a most penetrating fashion by setting it clearly in the context of contemporary problems and current criticism. His impatience with those who misread either deliberately or through grossly prejudiced or inexact scholarship is clearly justifiable, as is his attack on those who would attribute to Dewey motives and political attachments that are clearly inappropriate to the facts. His is not only a defense, but a clarification and interpretation of the Deweyan position by a serious philosopher who has a clear understanding of the subtle nuances of this thought. He properly sees Dewey's philosophy as a culmination of one major aspect of American educational thought, as a challenge that cannot simply be argued away but that must be met, since it represents in clear form the statement of the liberal, democratic, scientific strain in our thinking.

"The Philosophical Bases of the Experience Curriculum" is in some ways consistent with the approach taken by Hook, maintaining that the conflict between "progressives" and "traditionalists" has been carried on at the expense of both, and that possibilities for understanding and compromise between the two are truly possible if care can be taken to clarify the issues involved. The author argues that the misunderstanding of Dewey by his critics is certainly significant, but that the genuine understanding of the richness and subtlety of his position by his followers is of still greater import, and that a re-examination or "reconstruction" of his views, in a truly Deweyan fashion, would be in order.

The next section is concerned more particularly with progressive education as it is in evidence today, and Dewey's relation to it and his responsibility for it. M. I. Berger presents a balanced analysis of Dewey's actual views, particularly as they were stated in his late years, that led to the automatic equation between Deweyism and Progressive Education. He stresses Dewey's criticism of many facets of that movement and maintains that Dewey's view's are still applicable and valuable today. They require modification, but not rejection.

Albert Lynd essentially argues that the widespread *acceptance* of aspects of Deweyism is a direct result of a failure to understand his philosophy and that if it were understood it would be flatly rejected by the great majority of citizens. The kind of polemical attack presented by Lynd is typical of a great deal of anti-Deweyan criticism. There is a heavy emphasis here on Dewey's antagonism toward eternal truths, his criticism of fixed moral laws, his rejection of the traditional notion of the soul. From this treatment of some of the more non-conventional aspects of his basic thought, Lynd moves abruptly to practical deficiencies in the schools that are attributed to Dewey's progressive philosophy. Certainly Sidney Hook had this kind of critique in mind in his defense of Dewey against certain of his critics.

The final selection in the volume is by Jerome Bruner, and is appropriately entitled "After John Dewey, What?" Going back to Dewey's early and succinct statement of principles in "My Pedagogic Creed" of 1897, Bruner examines the extent to which these ideas and prescriptions are applicable to the present situation. Noting not only the enormous change in the world that has taken place since then, but also the many aspects of Dewey's views that have been accepted, at least in principle, Bruner presents a positive statement of contemporary educational needs that is in many ways consistent with Dewey's views and in others deeply antagonistic. Bruner's central point, and a very important one for current educational theory, is that Dewey's prescriptions were designed (consistent with his pragmatic principles) as an answer to the problems of a particular time and place. Some of these problems were theoretical, dealing with the scope, nature and function of educational theory itself. Others were practical, concerned as they were with specific educational conditions in a newly urbanized American society at the turn of the century. These theories, Bruner says, have served their purposes well, not only by contribution of valuable insights and truths that have been woven into American educational theory, but also because of the antagonistic movements and controversies that they have generated. But, Bruner says, it is time now to move away from our preoccupation with defending and attacking the Deweyan theory that was generated to meet the conditions of another society. We should store up the gains that have accrued, but move on to the real educational problems that now confront us precisely as a result of the gains that Dewey's philosophy have provided. Bruner's suggestions are very new, highly creative, and very important, for they point the way to an entirely new direction in educational theory and a whole new series of problems which Bruner feels we must confront.

These essays, then, cover a wide range of issues that arise from analysis of Dewey's educational theory. They are all critical in the sense that they evaluate that theory, and most do so in considerable depth. The hope is that they will stimulate a genuinely critical attitude on the part of the students of his philosophy so that the lasting value of many of the aspects of his thought can be understood and appreciated; so that his philosophy might be read anew, modified, and perhaps reconstructed in the light of our real contemporary problems; and so that this vital and flexible philosophy that has contributed so much might not degenerate, ironically, into a kind of formalism.

Providence, R. I.   REGINALD D. ARCHAMBAULT
September 1965

In Retrospect

———————————— ❧ ————————————

Personal Reminiscences of Dewey and My Judgment of His Present Influence

❧

William Heard Kilpatrick

My first personal contact with Prof. Dewey was in an 1898 summer course in education at the University of Chicago. However, I got little from the course; I was not ready for its thinking and I was not accustomed to Dewey's method of teaching. His practice, as I later learned, was to come to the class with a problem on his mind and sit before the class thinking out loud as he sought to bring creative thinking to bear on his problem.

A monograph by Dewey, "Interest as Related to Will," which I studied two years later under Charles DeGarmo, did have a deep and lasting effect on me and on my thinking. In it Dewey was analyzing a controversy as to the relative educative effect of "interest" and "effort" upon a pupil. The "interest" proponents had perverted the Herbartian doctrine of "interest" into a superficial "sugar-coating" device of "making things interesting"; the "effort" side, led by William T. Harris, charged that such "sugar-coating" would spoil children and was wrong anyway. What was needed was the building of character, and effort was essential to accomplishing this. To secure effort they proposed to coerce children into effort, by threats and punishment when necessary.

This selection originally appeared in *School and Society*, October, 1959. Professor Kilpatrick, who died in 1965, long served as Professor of Education at Teachers College, Columbia.

Dewey said, in effect, you are both wrong; by
sugar-coating you cannot make things effectively interesting: and coerced effort—forcing children to go
through motions without putting themselves into what
they do—will fail to build character. Especially you
have misunderstood the inherent relation between interest and effort; typically, personally felt interest is
the first stage of an on-going experience in which correlative personal effort is the effecting stage. Thus,
proper interest and proper effort cannot be opposed:
they are, in essence, correlative, the one leading to and
demanding the other.

At that time, I was a college professor of mathematics, but for several years I had been indulging in
education as a side interest. This Cornell experience of
Dewey, with its new insight into the educative process
as character-building, persuaded me to give up mathematics and center my interest henceforth on education as my life-work. For various good reasons I could
not act on my change of interest until 1907, when I
received a scholarship to Teachers College, Columbia.
Prof. Dewey was then teaching philosophy at Columbia; and for the next three years I took all his courses,
having decided meanwhile to major in philosophy of
education.

I entered upon my 1907 work with Prof. Dewey
thinking that in philosophy he still was a neo-Hegelian.
For a time, Dewey—along with many others—had followed this neo-Hegelian line; and I, too, after working
in philosophy at Johns Hopkins in 1895–96, had accepted it as my personal outlook. But now I found that
Dewey, stressing the conceptions of process, the continuity of nature, and the method of inductive science,
had built an entirely new philosophy, later called Experimentalism. As I worked with him during three constructive years, I gave up neo-Hegelianism and accepted

instead the new viewpoint, thereby gaining a fresh and invigorating outlook in life and thought.

From that time until Prof. Dewey's death in 1952, I had great satisfaction in the many contacts with him. Dewey read and approved the manuscript of my 1912 book, "The Montessori System Examined." When he himself had finished seven chapters of "Democracy and Education," he turned these over to me for criticism and to suggest other topics for completing the book. I was then teaching a course in Principles of Education; so I made a list of philosophic problems that troubled me in this course and turned them over to Dewey. At first he rejected my list, but later he redefined a number of the problems and these now appear as chapters in the completed book.

Another instance of personal experience with Dewey came after he had retired from Columbia and I meanwhile had accumulated considerable experience in teaching philosophy of education. He was offered a post as visiting professor in philosophy of education. Though his reputation as a creative thinker in both philosophy and philosophy of education was unsurpassed, he felt unsure as to certain practical details of the new post and accordingly came to me for advice. That I was glad to help needs no words here.

As to the origin of Dewey's educational ideas, some thought he had derived these from Rousseau and Froebel. I once asked him about this and he told me explicitly that he had not read either one until after he had formed his educational outlook. He did say in another connection, that he had got help in his educational thinking from Francis W. Parker, who was active in education in Chicago when Dewey came to the University of Chicago. As to the origin of Dewey's philosophy of life (and, consequently, of education), he himself makes it clear that he got his psychology from

William James. This means, as Dewey later brought out, that he and James were both deeply indebted to Darwin's "Origin of Species." It seems probable that from this source Dewey derived the conceptions of process, continuity of nature, and the method of inductive science referred to earlier. It also seems that certain important elements in Dewey's outlook—his belief in equality—came from the creative frontier background which he shared in his Vermont family in common with so many other Americans.

As to Dewey's comparative place in the history of philosophy, I place him next to Plato and Aristotle. As to his place in the history of philosophy of education, he is, as I see it, the greatest the world has yet beheld. As to his current influence in education, I place him in company with William James, Francis W. Parker, and Edward L. Thorndike—those who most efficiently have helped to shape our existent American educational thinking.

RELEVANT READING

Dewey, John, "From Absolutism to Experimentalism," in George P. Adams and William P. Montague, eds., *Contemporary American Philosophy: Personal Statements*. New York: The Macmillan Company, 1930.

Eastman, Max, "John Dewey." *Atlantic Monthly*, CLXVIII (December, 1941).

Geiger, George R., *John Dewey in Perspective*. New York: Oxford University Press, 1958.

Hook, Sidney, "Some Memories of John Dewey." *Commentary*, XIV (September, 1952).

Kilpatrick, William H., *Foundations of Method*. New York: The Macmillan Company, 1925.

—— *Source Book in the Philosophy of Education*. New York: The Macmillan Company, 1934.

—— "Dewey's Philosophy of Education." *Educational Forum*, XVII (January, 1953).

Schilpp, Paul A., ed., *The Philosophy of John Dewey*. The Library of Living Philosophers, Vol. I. Evanston and Chicago: Northwestern University, 1939.

The Historical Perspective

John Dewey and the Progressive-Education Movement, 1915–1952

❀

Lawrence A. Cremin

John Dewey had a story—it must have been a favorite of his—about "a man who was somewhat sensitive to the movements of things about him. He had a certain appreciation of what things were passing away and dying and of what things were being born and growing. And on the strength of that response he foretold some of the things that were going to happen in the future. When he was seventy years old the people gave him a birthday party and they gave him credit for bringing to pass the things he had foreseen might come to pass."[1] With characteristic modesty, Dewey told the story autobiographically, using it to describe his own place in the history of American life and thought. And granted the genuinely seminal character of his contribution, there was a measure of truth to his disclaimer.

Consider, for example, Dewey's relation to the early progressive-education movement; it provides an excellent case in point. We know that the movement arose during the 1890's as a many-sided protest against pedagogical narrowness and inequity. It was essentially pluralistic, often self-contradictory, and always related

This selection appeared originally in the *Teachers College Record*, Summer, 1959. Mr. Cremin is Professor of Education at Teachers College, Columbia.

[1] *John Dewey: The Man and His Philosophy* (Cambridge, Mass.: Harvard University Press, 1930), p. 174.

to broader currents of social and political progressivism. In the universities it appeared as part of a spirited revolt against formalism in philosophy, psychology, and the social sciences. In the cities it emerged as one facet of a larger program of social alleviation and municipal reform. Among farmers, it became the crux of a moderate, liberal alternative to radical agrarianism.

It was at the same time the "social education" demanded by urban settlement workers, the "schooling for country life" demanded by rural publicists, the vocational training demanded by businessmen's associations and labor unions alike, and the new techniques of instruction demanded by *avant garde* pedagogues. Like progressivism writ large, it compounded a fascinating congeries of seemingly disparate elements: the romanticism of G. Stanley Hall and the realism of Jacob Riis, the scientism of Joseph Mayer Rice and the reformism of Jane Addams. Its keynote was diversity, of protest, of protestor, of proposal, and of proponent; it was a diversity destined to leave its ineradicable mark on a half-century of educational reform.[2]

There were, needless to say, numerous attempts to portray this remarkable movement in its early decades; but nowhere is its extraordinary diversity more intelligently documented than in Dewey's volume *Schools of To-Morrow*, published in 1915 in collaboration with his daughter Evelyn.[3] Over the years, Dewey's continuing interest in pedagogical theory, his widely publicized work at the Laboratory School he and Mrs. Dewey had founded in 189., his reputation as a tough-minded analyst of pedagogical schemes, and his unfailing support of progressive causes had combined to make him increasingly an acknowledged spokesman

[2] See my essay, "The Progressive Movement in American Education: A Reappraisal," *Harvard Educational Review,* XXVII (Fall, 1957), pp. 251-270.

[3] John Dewey and Evelyn Dewey, *Schools of To-Morrow* (New York: Dutton, 1915).

of the progressive-education movement. *Schools of To-Morrow* did much to secure this image of him in the public mind. Within ten years the book had gone through fourteen printings, unusual for any book, unheard-of for a book about education.

Written neither as a textbook nor as a dogmatic exposition of "the new," the volume is designed "to show what actually happens when schools start out to put into practice, each in its own way, some of the theories that have been pointed to as the soundest and best ever since Plato."[4] More than anything, the Dewey of *Schools of To-Morrow* is the man "sensitive to the movement of things about him." The reader is treated to a fascinating collection of glimpses—into Marietta Johnson's Organic School at Fairhope, Alabama, Junius Meriam's experimental school at the University of Missouri, the Francis Parker School in Chicago, Caroline Pratt's Play School in New York, the Kindergarten at Teachers College, Columbia University, and certain public schools of Gary, Chicago, and Indianapolis. In each instance, the guiding educational theory is given and the techniques by which the theory is put into practice are described. The approach is essentially journalistic; Dewey's enterprise is to elucidate rather than to praise or criticize.

Yet there is a very special kind of reporting here, one that bears closer examination. Richard Hofstadter has observed that the Progressive mind was typically a journalistic mind, and that its characteristic contribution was that of a socially responsible reporter-reformer.[5] Certainly this was Dewey's central contribution in *Schools of To-Morrow*. For in addition to the who, the what, the when, and the where, Dewey gives us a succession of social whys that quickly trans-

4 *Ibid.,* Preface.
5 Richard Hofstadter, *The Age of Reform* (New York: Knopf, 1955), p. 185.

form a seemingly unrelated agglomeration of pedagogical experiments into the several facets of a genuine
social movement.

Merely as a record of what progressive education
actually was and what it meant to Dewey *circa* 1915,
the book is invaluable. The text abounds in vivid
descriptions of the physical education, the nature
studies, the manual work, the industrial training, and
the innumerable "socialized activities" in the schools
of tomorrow. There is exciting talk of more freedom
for children, of greater attention to individual growth
and development, of a new unity between education
and life, of a more meaningful school curriculum, of
a vast democratizing of culture and learning. Nowhere
is the faith and optimism of the progressive-education
movement more dramatically conveyed.

Moreover, as the analysis proceeds, Dewey's powers,
as a "socially responsible reporter-reformer" are soon
apparent. He points enthusiastically to the concern with
initiative, originality, and resourcefulness in the new
pedagogy, deeming these qualities central to the life of
a free society. He commends the breadth of the new
school programs, their attention to health, citizenship,
and vocation, arguing that such breadth is not only a
necessary adaptation to industrialism but an effort to
realize for the first time in history the democratic
commitment to equal educational opportunity. He sees
the new emphasis on "learning by doing" as a device
par excellence to narrow the gap between school and
life; and closeness to life is required "if the pupil is
to understand the facts which the teacher wishes him
to learn; if his knowledge is to be real, not verbal; if
his education is to furnish standards of judgment and
comparison."[6] Even more important, perhaps, a school
close to life sends into society men and women "intelligent in the pursuit of the activities in which they

[6] Dewey, *Schools of To-Morrow,* p. 294.

engage."[7] People educated in this way are inevitably agents of constructive social change, and the schools which educate them are thereby intimately bound to the larger cause of reform.[8] Indeed, it is this very tie that makes progressive education progressive!

Actually, the dialectic between Dewey the observer and Dewey the reformer is probably the most intriguing thing about the volume.[9] On the one hand, we know that many of the pedagogical experiments he describes grew up quite independently of his own theorizing.[10] On the other hand, we recognize much in *Schools of To-Morrow* that exemplifies the very things he himself was urging in pamphlets going back at least twenty years.[11] The only way to reconcile the two Deweys, it seems, is to return to his own disclaimer, that he really was "the man sensitive to the movement of things about him" and to the thesis that his most seminal contribution was to develop a body of pedagogical theory which could encompass the terrific diversity of the progressive-education movement. It is no coincidence that *Democracy and Edu-*

[7] *Ibid.*, p. 249.

[8] *Ibid.*, pp. 226–227.

[9] Actually, Evelyn Dewey visited the several schools and wrote the descriptive chapters of the volume; but no pun is intended by the phrase "Dewey the observer." The larger design of the book—both descriptive and analytical—is obviously the elder Dewey's.

[10] One need only check some of the independent accounts, for example, Marietta Johnson, "Thirty Years with an Idea" (Unpublished manuscript in the library of Teachers College, Columbia University, 1939), or Caroline Pratt, *I Learn from Children* (New York: Simon & Schuster, 1948).

[11] The ideas of *My Pedagogic Creed* (New York: E. L. Kellogg & Co., 1897), *The School and Society* (Chicago: University of Chicago Press, 1899), *The Child and the Curriculum* (Chicago: University of Chicago Press, 1902), and "The School as Social Center" (published in the National Education Association *Proceedings* for 1902) are particularly apparent. See Melvin C. Baker, *Foundations of John Dewey's Educational Theory* (New York: King's Crown Press, 1955) for an analysis of Dewey's pedagogical ideas prior to 1904.

cation came a year later and wove the diverse strands
of a quarter-century of educational protest and inno-
vation into an integral theory.[12] The later work has
since overshadowed *Schools of To-Morrow,* but the
two ought not to be read apart. One is as much the
classic of the early progressive-education movement as
the other. Their genius was to express a pedagogical
age. For their very existence, the movement was in-
fused with larger meaning and hence could never be
the same again.

World War I marks a great divide in the history of
progressive education. Merely the founding of the
Progressive Education Association in 1919 would have
changed the movement significantly, since what had
formerly been a rather loosely defined revolt against
academic formalism now gained a vigorous organiza-
tional voice.[13] But there were deeper changes, in the
image of progressivism itself, that were bound to influence the course and meaning of educational reform.

Malcolm Cowley, in his delightful reminiscence of
the twenties, *Exile's Return,* describes these changes
well. He notes insightfully that intellectual protest in
prewar years had mingled two quite different sorts of
revolt: bohemianism and radicalism. The one was essentially an individual revolt against puritan restraint;
the other, primarily a social revolt against the evils of
capitalism. World War I, he argues, brought a parting
of the ways. People were suddenly forced to decide
what kinds of rebels they were. If they were merely
rebels against puritanism, they could exist safely in Mr.

[12] John Dewey, *Democracy and Education* (New York: Macmillan, 1916).

[13] The organization was founded by a young reformist educator
named Stanwood Cobb, who had come under the influence of
Marietta Johnson. Dewey refused a number of early invitations to
associate himself with the group, but later served as its honorary
president. The best account of the Association's first years is given
in Robert Holmes Beck, "American Progressive Education, 1875–
1930" (Unpublished Ph.D. thesis, Yale University, 1942).

Wilson's world; if they were radicals, they had no place in it.[14]

Cowley's analysis provides a key to one of the important intellectual shifts of the twenties. With the end of the War, radicalism seemed no longer in fashion among the *avant garde*, particularly the artists and literati who flocked to the Greenwich Villages of New York, Chicago, and San Francisco. It did not die; it was merely eclipsed by a polyglot system of ideas which combined the doctrines of self-expression, liberty, and psychological adjustment into a confident, iconoclastic individualism that fought the constraints of Babbitry and the discipline of social reform as well. And just as prewar progressivism had given rise to a new educational outlook, one which cast the school as a lever of social change, so this postwar protest developed its own characteristic pedagogical argument: the notion that each individual has uniquely creative potentialities, and that a school in which children are encouraged freely to develop these potentialities is the best guarantee of a larger society truly devoted to human worth and excellence.

Now those who had read *Schools of To-Morrow* must certainly have recognized this essentially Rousseauan stance; it had been at the heart of several of the schools Dewey had described. Yet readers who had troubled to follow Dewey's argument to the end, and who had accepted his analysis incorporating Rousseau's insights into a larger social reformism, must have noted a curious difference of emphasis here.[15] For just as

[14] Malcolm Cowley, *Exile's Return* (New York: Norton, 1934), chap. ii. Henry F. May contends that the shift toward what Cowley calls bohemianism actually began well before the War. See "The Rebellion of the Intellectuals, 1912–1917," *American Quarterly*, VIII (Summer, 1956), pp. 114–126.

[15] The incorporation is most clearly evident in chapter xii of *Schools of To-Morrow*. See also Dewey's comments on Rousseau in chapters vii and ix of *Democracy and Education*.

radicalism seemed eclipsed in the broader protests of
the twenties, so it seemed to disappear from the progressive pedagogy of the decade.[16] For all intents and
purposes, the *avant garde* pedagogues expanded one
part of what progressive education had formerly meant
into its total meaning.

Nowhere is this transformation more clearly documented than in the characteristic exegesis of progressive education during the twenties, *The Child-
Centered School*.[17] Written by Harold Rugg and Ann
Shumaker in 1928, the volume attempts for the movement in its time what *Schools of To-Morrow* had done
a decade earlier. Its pages teem with pedagogical experiments illustrating the new articles of pedagogical
faith: freedom, child interest, pupil initiative, creative
self-expression, and personality development. And just
as Dewey had seen a central connection with democracy as the crux of the earlier movement, so Rugg and
Shumaker saw the relationship with the creative revolution of the twenties as the essential meaning of this
one. To grasp the significance of the child-centered
schools, they urged, one had to comprehend the his-
toric battle of the artist against the standardization, the
superficiality, and the commercialism of industrial
civilization. The key to the creative revolution of the
twenties was the triumph of self-expression, in art and
in education as well. Hence, in creative self-expression
they found the quintessential meaning of the progressive-education movement.

Dewey, of course, was not unaware of the continuing ferment in pedagogical circles. His interest in edu-

[16] Radicalism even tended to disappear from the pedagogical
formulations of many political radicals. See, for example, Agnes de
Lima, *Our Enemy the Child* (New York: New Republic, 1925),
chap. xii.

[17] Harold Rugg and Ann Shumaker, *The Child-Centered School*
(Yonkers-on-Hudson, New York: World Book, 1928).

cation persisted, but as the decade progressed he became less and less the sensitive observer and interpreter of the progressive-education movement and increasingly its critic. As early as 1926, for example, he attacked the studied lack of adult guidance in the *avant garde* schools with a sharpness uncommon in his writing. "Such a method," he observed, "is really stupid. For it attempts the impossible, which is always stupid; and it misconceives the conditions of independent thinking."[18] Freedom, he counselled, is not something given at birth; nor is it bred of planlessness. It is something to be achieved, to be systematically wrought out in co-operation with experienced teachers, knowledgeable in their own traditions. Baby, Dewey insisted, does not know best!

Two years later, the same year *The Child-Centered School* appeared, Dewey used the occasion of a major address before the Progressive Education Association to reiterate his point. "Progressive schools," he noted, "set store by individuality, and sometimes it seems to be thought that orderly organization of subject-matter is hostile to the needs of students in their individual character. But individuality is something developing and to be continuously attained, not something given all at once and ready-made."[19] Far from being hostile to the principle of individuality, he continued, some systematic organization of activities and subject matter is the only means for actually achieving individuality; and teachers, by virtue of their richer and fuller experience, have not only the right but the high obligation to assist students in the enterprise.

[18] His essay, originally published in the *Journal of the Barnes Foundation*, is reprinted in John Dewey *et al.*, *Art and Education* (Merion, Pa.: Barnes Foundation Press, 1929), pp. 32–40. p. 37.
[19] John Dewey, "Progressive Education and the Science of Education," *Progressive Education*, V (July-August-September, 1928), pp. 197–204. p. 201.

His strictures were not heeded, and in 1930 he leveled them even more vigorously in the concluding essay of a *New Republic* series evaluating a decade of progressive education.[20] The formalism and isolation of the conventional schoolroom had literally cried out for reform, he recalled. But the point of the progressive revolt had been not to rid the school of subject matter, but rather to build a new subject matter, as well organized as the old but having a more intimate relation to the experience of students. "The relative failure to accomplish this result indicates the one-sidedness of the idea of the 'child-centered' school."[21]

Then Dewey went on to a more pervasive criticism. Progressive schools, he conceded, had been most successful in furthering creativity in the arts. But this accomplishment, however much it contributed to private sensibilities, had hardly met either the social or the aesthetic needs of a democratic-industrial society. A truly progressive education, he concluded, "requires a searching study of society and its moving forces. That the traditional schools have almost wholly evaded consideration of the social potentialities of education is no reason why progressive schools should continue the evasion, even though it be sugared over with aesthetic refinements. The time ought to come when no one will be judged to be an educated man or woman who does not have insight into the basic forces of industrial and urban civilization. Only schools which take the lead in bringing about this kind of education can claim to be progressive in any socially significant sense."[22]

[20] John Dewey, "How Much Freedom in New Schools?" *New Republic,* LXIII (July 9, 1930), pp. 204–206. The decade to which the *New Republic* refers is, of course, 1919–1929. The implication, that progressive education really began with the founding of the Progressive Education Association, is oft-repeated but erroneous.

[21] *Ibid.,* p. 205.

[22] Dewey, "How Much Freedom in New Schools?" p. 206.

Dewey's comments seemed particularly *à propos* in the summer of 1930. Already the depression which was to envelop the nation and become the central fact of the thirties was very much in evidence. Breadlines were common in the industrial cities, and women could be seen raking through community refuse heaps as soon as garbage trucks departed. Suddenly radicalism was no longer passé; it was bohemianism that appeared a little out of date.[23] Socially conscious notions of progressive education, disparaged by the *avant garde* of the twenties as "social efficiency," were now very much to the point.[24]

It should be no surprise that Dewey's formulation of the meaning of progressivism in education came once again to the fore. Early in 1932 he accepted membership on a yearbook commission of the National Society of College Teachers of Education dedicated to producing a statement of philosophy of education appropriate to the times. The volume which emerged, *The Educational Frontier*, is, like *The Child-Centered School*, the characteristic progressivist statement of its decade. And while its formulations are essentially collaborative, Dewey's own views are clearly discernible in two chapters he wrote jointly with his student, John L. Childs.[25]

The Dewey of these chapters is now the vigorous proponent. His plea is for an educational program conceived in the broadest terms, one which has "definite reference to the needs and issues which mark and divide our domestic, economic, and political life in the

[23] Cowley's Epilogue in the 1951 reissue of *Exile's Return* is an interesting commentary on this point.

[24] The common cry was that Dewey had been too much the rationalist to develop an adequate theory of creativity. See, for example, *The Child-Centered School*, pp. iv; 324–325.

[25] William H. Kilpatrick, ed., *The Educational Frontier* (New York: D. Appleton-Century, 1933). Dewey actually wrote chapters ii and ix, though as joint efforts with Childs. See also "The Crucial Role of Intelligence," *Social Frontier*, I (February, 1935), pp. 9–10.

generation of which we are a part."[26] As with his educational outlook from the beginning, his call is for a school close to life, one that will send into society people able to understand it, to live intelligently as part of it, and to change it to suit their visions of the better life. Once again, he sees changes through education as "correlative and interactive" with changes through politics. "No social modification, slight or revolutionary, can endure except as it enters into the action of a people through their desires and purposes. This introduction and perpetuation are effected by education."[27]

Dewey held essentially to this position throughout the stormy thirties. To George Counts's provocative question "Dare the school build a new social order?" Dewey replied that in an industrial society with its multiplicity of political and educative agencies, the school could never be the main determinant of political, intellectual, or moral change.[28] "Nevertheless," he continued, "while the school is not a sufficient condition, it is a necessary condition of *forming the understanding and the dispositions* that are required to maintain a genuinely changed social order."[29] It would be revolution enough, Dewey once told an NEA audience, were educators to begin to recognize the fact

[26] *Ibid.*, p. 36.

[27] *Ibid.*, p. 318.

[28] See George S. Counts, *Dare the School Build a New Social Order?* (New York: John Day Co., 1932). The tension between bohemianism and radicalism within the progressive-education movement is dramatically portrayed by Counts in a 1932 address to the Progressive Education Association, "Dare Progressive Education Be Progressive?" *Progressive Education,* IX (April, 1932), pp. 257–263.

[29] John Dewey, "Education and Social Change," *Social Frontier,* III (May, 1937), pp. 235–238. Italics mine. See also "Can Education Share in Social Reconstruction?" *Social Frontier,* I (October, 1934), pp. 11–12.

of social change and to act upon that recognition in the schools.[30]

Dewey steadfastly opposed indoctrination in the form of the inculcation of fixed social beliefs. But he did contend that for schools to be progressive, teachers would have to select the newer scientific, technological, and cultural forces producing changes in the old order, estimate their outcomes if given free play, and see what could be done to make the schools their ally.[31] To some, of course, this was as crass a form of indoctrination as any; and Dewey was criticized on the one hand by those who insisted that his notions would cast the school into an indefensible presentism at the expense of traditional values and verities, and on the other by those in the progressive camp who maintained that any social guidance by adults was really an unwarranted form of imposition.

Dewey replied to both groups in what was destined to be his most important pedagogical work of the thirties, *Experience and Education.* The volume is really a restatement of aspects of his educational outlook in the context of the criticisms, distortions, and misunderstandings which had grown up over two decades. There is little fundamentally new, except perhaps the tone. Progressive educators, he suggests, should begin to think "in terms of Education itself rather than in terms of some 'ism about education, even such an 'ism as 'progressivism.' For in spite of itself any movement that thinks and acts in terms of an 'ism becomes so involved in reaction against other 'isms that it is

[30] John Dewey, "Education for a Changing Social Order," National Education Association *Proceedings,* 1934, pp. 744–752.

[31] Dewey, "Education and Social Change"; and "Education, Democracy, and Socialized Economy," *Social Frontier,* V (December, 1938), pp. 71–72. The latter article deals with an exchange between John L. Childs and Boyd H. Bode in the previous issue of *Social Frontier.*

unwittingly controlled by them. For it then forms
its principles by reaction against them instead of by a
comprehensive constructive survey of actual needs,
problems, and possibilities."[32] By 1938, Dewey the
sensitive observer could already note, probably with a
measure of sadness, that the movement was devoting
too much of its energy to internecine ideological conflict and too little, perhaps, to the advancement of its
own cause.

Frederic Lilge, in a perceptive essay he recently published in a volume honoring Robert Ulich, contends
that Dewey's pedagogical progressivism embodies a
fundamental inconsistency which Dewey never really
resolves.[33] A theory which seems to harmonize the
school with the larger social environment, Lilge argues,
and which casts the school as a lever of reform, inevitably faces a twofold difficulty: first in determining
which social goals to serve in the school; and second,
in deciding whether or not to embark on an ever
broader program of political reform outside the school.
Thus, "Dewey was confronted by two equally re-
pellent alternatives: pursuing his basic aim of adjusting
the schools to the social environment, he could integrate them with institutions and practices whose underlying values he rejected; or he could attempt to
withdraw them from being thus corrupted, but at the
cost of sacrificing that closeness to actual life which
it was one of the main aims of his educational philosophy to establish."[34] Lilge contends that Dewey accepted neither, and that the thirties saw him and a

[32] John Dewey, *Experience and Education* (New York: Macmillan, 1938), pp. vi–vii.
[33] Frederic Lilge, "Politics and the Philosophy of Education," in
Liberal Traditions in Education, George Z. F. Bereday, ed. (Cambridge, Mass.: Graduate School of Education, Harvard University,
1958), pp. 27–49.
[34]*Ibid.,* p. 29.

number of influential followers increasingly thrust into a clearly political program of reform, both via the schools and outside them. Their manifesto was Counts's pamphlet, *Dare the School Build a New Social Order;* their statement of educational principles was *The Educational Frontier;* their intellectual organ was the *Social Frontier*, a journal which appeared regularly in the decade following 1934.

Now Lilge himself grants that his analysis is far more relevant to some of Dewey's disciples than to Dewey himself. Even so, some clarification is needed. For to pose the dilemma in the first place is to misread the relationship between progressive education and progressivism writ large, particularly as Dewey perceived it. Dewey had no illusions about the school changing society on its own; that educational and political reform would have to go hand in hand was the progressive view from the beginning.[35] Nor did the notion of adjusting the school to society imply that the school would have to accommodate itself to all institutions and practices. Dewey wanted schools to use the stuff of reality to educate men and women intelligent about reality. His notion of adjustment was an adjustment *of* conditions, not *to* them, a remaking of existing conditions, not a mere remaking of self and individual to fit into them.[36] And as for the corrupting influence of life itself, Dewey was no visionary; the problem for him was not to build *the perfect society* but *a better society*. To this he thought a school that educated for intelligence about reality could make a unique contribution.

Dewey restated these faiths in the introductory essay he wrote for Elsie Clapp's 1952 volume, *The*

[35] Dewey makes the point on page 226 of *Schools of To-Morrow* and in Article V of *My Pedagogic Creed*.

[36] This is a central point in view of contemporary attacks on Dewey. See *The Educational Frontier*, p. 312.

Use of Resources in Education; it is probably his last major statement on education.[37] Once again, he returns to the role of sensitive observer. "In the course of more than half a century of participation in the theory and practice of education," he writes, "I have witnessed many successes and many failures in what is popularly known as 'progressive education,' but is also known as 'the new education,' 'modern education,' and so on." He sees the triumph of the movement in the changed life-conditions of the American classroom, in a greater awareness of the needs of the growing human being, in the warmer personal relations between teachers and students. But as with all reform victories, he sees attendant dangers. No education is progressive, he warns, unless it is making progress. And he observes somewhat poignantly that in schools and colleges across the country, progressive education has been converted into a set of fixed rules and procedures "to be applied to educational problems externally, the way mustard plasters, for example, are applied." If this ossification continues, he fears progressive education will end up guilty of the very formalism it sought to correct, a formalism "fit for the foundations of a totalitarian society and, for the same reason, fit to subvert, pervert and destroy the foundations of a democratic society."

"For the creation of democratic society," he concludes, "we need an educational system where the process of moral-intellectual development is in practice as well as in theory a cooperative transaction of inquiry engaged in by free, independent human beings who treat ideas and the heritage of the past as means and methods for the further enrichments of life, quantitatively and qualitatively, who use the good attained for the discovery and establishment of some-

[37] Elsie Ripley Clapp, *The Use of Resources in Education* (New York: Harper, 1952), pp. vii–xi.

thing better." Dewey's sentence is involved, complex, and overly long; but it embodies the essence of the movement as he saw it. Those who would understand progressive education would do well to ponder it, as would those who set out to build today's schools of tomorrow.

RELEVANT READING

Cremin, Lawrence A., "The Origins of Progressive Education." *Educational Forum*, XXIV (January, 1960).

———— "The Progressive Movement in American Education: A Perspective." *Harvard Educational Review*, XXVII (Fall, 1957).

———— *The Transformation of the School: Progressivism in American Education 1876–1957.* New York: Alfred A. Knopf, Inc., 1961.

———— "What Happened to Progressive Education?" *Teachers College Record*, LXI (October, 1959).

Kelley, Truman L., "The Passing of the Progressive Education Association." *School and Society*, LX (December, 1944).

John Dewey's Challenge to Education

❧

Oscar Handlin

DEWEY AND THE PROBLEMS OF EDUCATION

It was the achievement of John Dewey to have couched his criticism of the divorce between experience and education in more meaningful terms. His practical con-

These selections appeared originally in *John Dewey's Challenge to Education,* 1959 (Copyright © 1959 by Harper & Brothers). Mr. Handlin is Professor of History at Harvard University.

tact with the problems of the schools of the 1880's and
1890's stimulated his philosophical inquiries into the
nature of knowledge; and his understanding of the
learning process supplied a theoretical basis to his
views on proper pedagogy. The development of his
ideas was thus meaningfully related to the context of
the times in which he lived.

When Dewey came as instructor to the University
of Michigan in 1884, he brought with him intellectual
attitudes shaped by two forces. His early upbringing
in Vermont had been permissive to the point of chaos;
the most valuable lessons he had learned had been outside the classroom and independently carried forth.
His own training had thus been almost casual and had
certainly been free of the rigidity to be imposed on
American schools after 1870. Recollections of his experience as a student no doubt influenced his later
critical view of what education was becoming in the
last quarter of the nineteenth century.

His philosophical background also raised questions
with regard to current assumptions. From his graduate
work under George S. Morris at Johns Hopkins he
carried away a commitment to Hegelian idealism,
which nurtured his hostility to dualisms of every sort
and left him dubious as to the validity of all such
dichotomies as those between education or culture
and society or life.[1]

But at Michigan, Dewey's formal philosophical views
and his personal memories were challenged by the
necessities of instruction and by his immersion in the
life of a community. To make his ideas comprehensible
to the young men and women in his classrooms was
but a fraction of his task. In addition, he had to be
aware of the relationship of his work to the world

[1] Sidney Hook, *John Dewey, an Intellectual Portrait* (New York:
John Day, 1939), p. 13; Jerome Nathanson, *John Dewey* (New
York: Charles Scribner's, 1951), pp. 10 ff.; Max Eastman, *Heroes
I Have Known* (New York: Simon and Schuster, 1942), pp. 278 ff.

about him; and as a member of the faculty of a state university, he also had to concern himself with the problems of the public school system related to it. President Angell always regarded it as one of the chief duties of the university "to keep in close touch with the state system of public education." That preoccupation was reflected in Dewey's proposal to publish a general "Thought News"; and it emerged also in his earliest books, the core of which was analysis of the ways of knowing. The title of the volume in which he collaborated in 1889 was significant: *Applied Psychology: An Introduction to the Principles and Practices of Education.*[2]

His marriage in 1886 and the move to Chicago in 1894 added to the weight of the practical considerations in the development of his thought. The intellectual associations at the exciting new university were undoubtedly stimulating; but the exposure to the immediate problems of teaching in a great and expanding metropolis were fully as much so. Experiments in new education were already in progress in Chicago; and the Deweys at the Experimental School undoubtedly profited from them. But it is, in any case, clear that the main outlines of their work were set up on a pragmatic rather than a theoretical basis. That is, Dewey began to treat the problems of education not from an abstract, previously defined position of what ought ideally to be, but rather from a concrete estimate of deficiencies that actually existed.[3]

---

[2] Willinda Savage, "John Dewey and 'Thought News,'" Claude Eggertsen, ed., *Studies in the History of Higher Education in Michigan* (Ann Arbor: 1950), pp. 12 ff.; A. S. Whitney, *History of the Professional Training of Teachers at the University of Michigan* (Ann Arbor: G. Wahr, 1931), pp. 34, 35; Eastman, *op. cit.,* pp. 291, 292.

[3] P. A. Schilpp, ed., *The Philosophy of John Dewey* (New York: Northwestern University, 1951), p. 452; Katherine Mayhew, *The Dewey School* (New York: D. Appleton-Century, 1936).

The systematic exploration of these problems did not follow until later. The first extensive exposition of Dewey's position came in the lectures collected as *The School and Society* (1899), a work which was still largely critical and negative. A fuller analysis appeared seventeen years later in *Democracy and Education*. But the general propositions enunciated in that work rested upon a very careful case by case study of particular experiments in the new education. Dewey's general conclusions were thus the products of more than twenty years of experience. His ideas were not formulated in the abstract but through the encounter with the conditions of learning in the United States in the closing decades of the nineteenth century.

The necessity for grappling with a development that had divorced the school and its culture from society and its life was an irritant that compelled Dewey to define his ideas on education. Those ideas were integrally related to his comprehensive conceptions of the character of knowledge, the mind, human nature, the experimental process, and the values of democracy. As he clarified his thoughts on education he also refined his views on these more general philosophical issues.[4]

But his conceptions also had a pragmatic attractiveness that converted many Americans who did not accept or were unfamiliar with the wider implications of his philosophy. His ideas were persuasive because they revealed the evident weaknesses of the schools as they were.

[4] See, in general, G. R. Geiger, *John Dewey in Perspective* (New York: Oxford University Press, 1958); Morton White, *Social Thought in America* (Boston: Viking, 1957), pp. 94 ff.; Schilpp, *op. cit.*, pp. 419 ff.

WHAT WAS WRONG WITH AMERICAN EDUCATION

The realm of the classroom in the 1890's was totally set off from the experience of the child who inhabited it. The teachers' lessons encrusted by habit, the seats arranged in formal rows, and the rigid etiquette of behavior all emphasized the difference between school and life. Hence learning consisted of the tedious memorization of data without a meaning immediately clear to the pupil.

Dewey, whose own education as a boy was free of all such rigidity, objected strenuously that these conditions stifled the learning process, for they prevented the student from relating his formal studies to his own development as a whole person.

The educator therefore had to narrow the distance between the classroom and the world outside it. Society was changing rapidly under the impact of urbanization and industrialization, and not always for the better. But the teacher ought not therefore pretend that his pupils still walked along the lanes of an eighteenth-century village back to a rustic farmhouse. He had to take account of the city streets and of the American home as it actually was.[5]

The educator could end the school's isolation by pulling it into a closer relationship with the family and the community. Awareness of the homes, the neighborhood environment, and the business and professional life about it would enable the school to function more effectively and also to widen its influence. By recognizing the unity of the child's experience, it could communicate more directly with him and at the same time break down the pernicious "division into cul-

[5] John Dewey, *The School and Society* (Chicago: University of Chicago Press, 1899), pp. 18–22.

tured people and workers." It would then cease to be
alien and hostile in the eyes of its students and become
instead a natural part of their habitat within which
they sought satisfaction of their own needs.[6]

In such schools, the "subject matter in history and
science and art" could be so presented that it would
have "a positive value and a real significance in the
child's own life." What was taught would justify itself
because it answered questions the student himself asked.
He would not be forced to study the map to learn
what the world was like; but exploring the world
about him, would come to wonder how it looked on
the map. History and literature would cease to be the
elegant furnishings of an abstract culture; the pupil
would be drawn to them out of his own desire to
know himself and his origins. Mathematics would no
longer be a burdensome exercise in mental discipline
but would be sought as a practical way of managing
quantities.[7]

Instruction, under such conditions, could be carried
forward as a succession of direct experiences on the
child's part. From Rousseau, Dewey had learned that
education was not something to be forced upon youth.
It involved rather a process of growth antedating the
pupil's admission to the school and extending beyond
his departure from it. In teaching it was essential
always to take account of the conditions of learning,
to impart the ability to read, to write, and to use
figures intelligently in terms that were themselves
meaningful and real. That meant at the lower grades
an emphasis on activities over abstractions, not as ends
in themselves but as means of evoking stimulating
questions.[8]

[6] *Ibid.*, pp. 38, 82 ff.

[7] *Ibid.*, p. 113.

[8] E. C. Moore, "John Dewey's Contributions to Educational
Theory," *John Dewey, the Man and His Philosophy* (Cambridge,
Mass.: Harvard University Press, 1930), p. 23.

Learning would then become incidental to the process of dealing with authentic situations. Children who
played at making things readily learned to weave, but
in doing so began to wonder how cotton and wool
came to be formed into their own garments. Those
who had practice in electing a class president found it
natural to inquire how the city elected a mayor.

The school was thus not simply to pander to a
child's liking for interesting activities. It was to select
those which led him on to a widening of significant
achievements. Knowledge of geography, government,
history, and arithmetic was acquired through the continual reconstruction of the student's own experiences.
As he absorbed the significance of what he did, he
was able to direct his attention to ever broader and
more meaningful subjects. Furthermore, interest in the
achievement of a practical end could steadily be transformed into interest in the process, that is into "thinking things out" intellectually or theoretically. The
whole of education could thus be conceived as the
process of learning to think through the solution of
real problems.[9]

A school firmly oriented in the world of its pupils
could dispense with discipline through the external
force of keeping order. Children whose interest was
actively engaged in their studies did not need policing.
They could be permitted more than the usual amount
of freedom, not for the purpose of relaxing real discipline, but to make possible the assumption of larger
and less artificial responsibilities, the performance of
which would evoke order from within.[10]

The establishment of voluntary patterns of obedience not only facilitated the teacher's task; it also
emphasized that which was most important in educa-

---

[9] Geiger, *op. cit.,* pp. 197–198; Hook, *op. cit.,* pp. 177 ff.
[10] Dewey, *op. cit.,* pp. 124, 125; John Dewey, *Democracy and
Education* (New York: Macmillan, 1916), p. 138.

tion—its moral purpose. "All the aims and manners
which are desirable in education are themselves moral.
Discipline, natural development, culture, social efficiency, are moral traits—marks of a person who is a
worthy member of that society which it is the business
of education to further." Education was not simply a
preparation for what would later be useful. It was
more, "getting from the present the degree and kind
of growth there is in it." From the very start therefore the child would become acquainted with, and
through his life learn ever better, the relationship of
knowledge to conduct. That was the most worthy
function of his schooling.[11]

THE RELEVANCE OF DEWEY'S CRITIQUE

Dewey's central conceptions of education are thus
directly related to criticisms of the system that had
developed in the United States between the time when
he had ended his own schooling in Vermont and the
time when he moved to Chicago. The conditions that
evoked his revolt have changed radically since 1894;
yet his comments have by no means lost their timeli-
ness.

In some sixty years since the experimental school in
Chicago opened its doors, John Dewey's ideas have
had a profound effect upon American education.
Despite the occasional errors in their application to
practice and despite the distortions by uncritical
enthusiasts, the schools have profited immensely from
his influence.

There have been failings, but due largely through a
disregard of the spirit of Dewey's intentions. In the
hands of mediocre or incompetent teachers, new tech-

[11] Dewey, *Democracy and Education,* pp. 362, 417; Dewey,
School and Society, pp. 124, 125; Dewey, *Reconstruction in Philosophy* (New York: Holt, 1920), pp. 183–185.

niques have sometimes become ends in themselves.
Dewey valued the experiment and the laboratory as
means through which the pupil could learn by discovery. But when instruction is so routinized that the
student knows from the manual what he will find
before he puts his eye to the lens, the microscope has
added nothing to his education. There is no point to
substituting modern for ancient languages if dull
teachers make one as dead as the other.

The danger of the abuse of techniques as ends in
themselves has certainly been heightened by the tendency in many states to emphasize method over content in the preparation of the teacher. Yet Dewey
always insisted that method could not be divorced
from content. The subject matter and the means of
communicating it were inextricably bound together;
and a successful performance depended on the mastery
of both. It is ironic now to find Dewey often blamed
in retrospect for the proliferation of empty courses
in "education" and for the "certification racket" that
makes completion of a formal quota of methods courses
the prerequisite to teacher licensing. "Consider the
training schools of teachers," he wrote in 1899. "These
occupy at present a somewhat anomalous position for
thus they are isolated from the higher subject matter
of scholarship, since, upon the whole, their object has
been to train persons *how* to teach, rather than *what*
to teach."[12]

Much of Dewey's writing was addressed to the
problems of the elementary school, which in his day
were most pressing. But neither at that nor at any other
level did he regard familiarity with techniques as an
alternative to command of the substance of subject
matter. The two were inseparable at any level, for
each acquired meaning from its relationship to the
other.

[12] Dewey, *School and Society,* p. 80.

Insofar as they are focused upon these abuses the complaints of the critics of Deweyism have a measure of validity. But the accusation that progressive education has kept Johnny from learning how to read or how to use a slide rule is unfounded and dangerous. It tends also to obscure the genuine improvements that have emanated from his influence.

In 1928, in an article on Soviet education, John Dewey pointed to the significance of the Russian achievement—far earlier than his detractors of thirty years later. But he did not then take, nor would be now have taken, technological proficiency or advances in rocketry as a test of the excellence of an educational system. He was certainly not impressed in the 1930's by the accomplishments of the Nazis in the same fields. Nor would he have overlooked in any comparison the counter-balancing achievements of our own educational system in medicine, in the peaceful branches of science, and in the humanities.[13]

The crucial test, rather, was the extent to which education served as a vital instrument teaching the individual to behave in the world about him. In his own society, Dewey warned that "academic and scholastic, instead of being titles of honor are becoming terms of reproach." He took that as a measure of the isolation of the schools and the negligence of the culture; and he feared that without an immediate reform schools would become empty and ineffective and the culture would be weakened from within. That accounted for the urgency with which he wrote.[14]

Dewey did not intend that his criticisms should become the creed of a sect or party; and he was uncom-

[13] John Dewey, "Impressions of Soviet Russia IV: What Are the Russian Schools Doing?; V: New Schools for a New Era," *New Republic*, LVII (1928), pp. 64–67, 91–94; Schilpp, *op. cit.*, p. 471.

[14] Dewey, *School and Society*, p. 36.

fortable when the label "Progressive" was attached
to his ideas. He directed his revolt not against tradition
but against a rather recent development—the gap
created by the inability of Americans to adjust their
conceptions of education and culture to the terms of
the changing world about them. Unwilling to limit the
scope of either education or culture by the lines of an
artificial definition, he insisted upon broadening both
by re-establishing their relationship to life.[15]

Late in life, reflecting upon the developments of a
half-century, he made this clear, when he defined the
new education as hostility to "imposition from above,"
to "learning from texts and teacher," to "acquisition
of isolated skills and techniques by drill" to "preparation for a more or less remote future" and to "static
aims and materials." Against those aspects of the
school of the late nineteenth century he had called
for the "expression and cultivation of individuality,"
for "learning through experience," and for "acquaint-
ance with an ever-changing world."[16]

That much can be ascribed to the reaction against
the trends of the 1880's and 1890's. But Dewey had no
intention of proceeding entirely upon a basis of rejection. "When external authority is rejected," he
pointed out in another connection, "it does not follow
that all authority should be rejected, but rather that
there is need to search for a more effective source of
authority." In his times, the disjunction between the
school and society had enshrined external and arbitrary
authority in American education. His revolt, which
is comprehensible in terms of his times, aimed to end

[15] R. F. Butts and L. A. Cremin, *History of Education in Amer-
ican Culture* (New York: Holt, 1953), pp. 343 ff., 384; L. A.
Cremin, "Revolution in American Secondary Education," *Teachers
College Record*, LVI (1955), pp. 301 ff.

[16] John Dewey, *Experience and Education* (New York: Macmillan, 1938), p. 56.

that disjunction and sweep away that authority as a
step in the reconstruction of education on a sounder
basis.

RELEVANT READING

Blau, Joseph L., "John Dewey and American Social Thought."
    Teachers College Record, LXI (December, 1959).
Dewey, John, "Authority and Resistance to Social Change."
    School and Society, XLIV (October, 1936).
—— "The Democratic Faith and Education." *Antioch Re-
    view*, IV, (June, 1944).
Handlin, Oscar, "American Secondary Education at the Dewey
    Centennial." *Frontiers of Secondary Education*, IV. Syra-
    cuse University, School of Education, 1959.
—— "Rejoinder to Critics of John Dewey." *New York Times
    Magazine* (June 15, 1958).

The Quest for Unity

John Dewey's War on Dualism—

ITS BEARING ON TODAY'S EDUCATIONAL PROBLEMS

❦

Philip H. Phenix

The philosophy of John Dewey was created out of reflection on the conditions and problems of a rapidly changing civilization. It should not be surprising, then, if its concepts, spirit, and methods were to prove singularly resistant to obsolescence. The situation in culture generally, and in education particularly, has altered radically in many respects since Dewey did the major part of his work, yet his insights remain as relevant today as when he first proposed them.

In what follows I intend to discuss one of the central themes of Dewey's philosophy—his war on dualism —and to illustrate its continuing importance by using it in an analysis of several current educational issues.

All thinking depends upon the discrimination of differences. Knowledge and intelligent activity require the making of distinctions among things, events, qualities, quantities, or relations. These differences are expressed in language by means of pairs of contrasting concepts, such as hot and cold, large and small, past and present, individual and group. Such concepts are *abstractions* which are useful for certain limited purposes. Sometimes their abstract and limited character is lost sight of, and the pairs of opposites are treated as independent and mutually exclusive realities, i.e.,

This selection originally appeared in *Phi Delta Kappan,* October, 1959. Mr. Phenix is Professor of Education at Columbia Teachers College.

as *dualities*. When they are so regarded, they become a source of intellectual confusion and misguided conduct, through neglect of the concrete unities from which the abstractions have been drawn.

In modern times Descartes is usually regarded as the fountainhead of dualism. His absolute distinction between mind and body in large measure set the stage for the philosophic history of the past three hundred years. Philosophy, as Whitehead observed, is the critic of abstractions, and there is no better exemplification of this dictum than the effort of modern philosophers to find a way out of the tangle of problems generated by the Cartesian absolutized abstractions.

John Dewey was much concerned with the mischief wrought by dualism. In this he was at one with the philosophic idealists—particularly Hegel—whom he had studied early in his intellectual career, but whom he transcended and transformed in the light of experimental science and evolutionary naturalism. Even a casual reader of Dewey's writings cannot but be impressed by his recurrent attacks upon what he regards as illegitimate oppositions, such as knowing *vs*. doing, freedom *vs*. authority, body *vs*. mind, nature *vs*. nurture, the child *vs*. the curriculum, objective *vs*. subjective, emotion *vs*. intellect, man *vs*. nature, the fine arts *vs*. the useful arts, heredity *vs*. environment, and so on through a very long list.

Dewey never denied that such polar abstractions have a certain logic and may mark intellectual distinctions valid within recognized limits and for specified purposes. What he did oppose was the neglect of the more important connections and relationships which the solidification of these general categories encouraged. The restoration of a proper integral perspective thus became a central objective of Dewey's philosophic mission.

•   •   •

How did Dewey propose to redeem our ways of thinking from the snares of dualism? What remedy did he offer for the difficulties caused by trying to keep separate the inseparable? I shall suggest four important concepts in Dewey's thought which exemplify his approach to the unity which saves us from dualism.

Nature. Dewey taught that there is but one world, the all-comprehending spacio-temporal complex which we call nature. This world of nature is one in two senses: first, in that there is no super-natural or extra-natural realm beside, beyond, above, or underlying it; and second, in that this natural world is not itself divided into distinct and mutually exclusive realms, such as the material and the mental or the physical and the spiritual. All that is, is in nature and of nature. Inanimate matter, living organisms, human beings with intelligence, social institutions and culture—all are realities of nature. Human beings are just as natural as plants, animals, or rocks, and the operation of creative human intelligence is just as natural as cellular growth or planetary motion.

As a critical naturalist—not a reductive materialist —Dewey rejected the "bifurcation of nature" implicit in dualistic world views. Against the prevailing estrangements, infidelities, and divorces in much modern thought he persistently warned, "What nature hath joined together let not man put asunder!"

Experience. A human being is an organism which by virtue of intelligence is uniquely equipped to make appropriate adaptive adjustments within the constantly changing and challenging world. The happenings which affect human beings and the actions which they consciously effect in response constitute the domain of experience. That is, to say, experience is the manifold of human undergoings and doings within the natural world, insofar as they are consciously perceived and personally recognized and appropriated. It is all meaningful, or significant, acts upon and by human beings.

Dewey insisted that all thought must refer to experience, that all valid knowledge and sound practical judgment must proceed from the analysis of experience. Distinctions and contrasts may be made by thought, but always from within the encompassing unity of experience. Ideas are worthless when they lose connection with the actual struggle of human beings to understand and control themselves and their environment. Hence productive thinking about human problems should proceed, not from ready-made, *a priori* abstractions, but from real situations in which people try to solve problems and seek for meaning in what they undergo and direction for what they perform.

Interaction. Dewey did not escape from dualism into metaphysical monism. He did not assimilate nature to Idea, like the objective idealists, nor reduce everything to dead matter, like the materialists. Turning his back on metaphysical speculation, he accepted the pluralism of common sense which regards the world as containing many different and distinct things and kinds of things. However, nature is forever changing, and this dynamism results from an unending process of interaction. Things act and react upon one another, and in so doing are reciprocally transformed. This interactive relationship between things constitutes a bond of unity which contradicts any absolute separation or isolation imposed by dualistic categories.

Like other denizens of nature, human beings are engaged in continual interaction with other elements in their human and non-human environment. People, like non-human beings, are what they are through interaction. Experience is social, to the core. The quality of experience is a consequence of the character of the interactions which have occurred.

Continuity. Dualism presupposes the idea of discontinuity—of sharp breaks, unrelieved contrasts, absolute distinctions, and unbridgeable gulfs. In place of this idea Dewey substituted the principle of continuity. All things develop by a process of change which proceeds continuously from one point to the next. For example, mind is not utterly separate and distinct from body; rather, mental activity is continuous with other modes of organic adaptive behavior and is merely characteristic of mankind as the highest species in the scale of continuous evolutionary development. Again, ideals are not mysterious revelations from an extra-natural realm; rather, they are extensions and purifications of goals suggested by actual experience within nature. Thus, ideality and actuality are continuous with one another.

The scientific method of causal explanation further illustrates the principle of continuity. An event is intelligible only in the light of relevant antecedent happenings and circumstances. Things are what they are by virtue of a particular causal path by which they have continuously travelled into the present. So it is with the future. Ends or goals are empty abstractions apart from a consideration of the means by which present actuality may be continuously transformed into the purposed future. Nor is the end thus reached really a conclusion; the continuity of process reveals the so-called end as a new beginning, as a means to the realization of still further aims.

Nature, experience, interaction, and continuity are, then, four unitive concepts by which Dewey waged war on dualism. With these and other conceptual tools he carried the fight into many of the major areas of human concern, such as government, economic life, social organizations, art, morals, and religion. Most significant of all, of course, was his contribution to educational theory and practice. In thought and conduct education has long been plagued by dualisms, and against these Dewey conducted many a spirited campaign.

In the remaining paragraphs I intend to analyze briefly five important contemporary issues in education in the spirit of Dewey's attack on dualism. I hope to illustrate thereby the continuing pertinence of his thought to our educational perplexities.

I. STUDENT MOTIVATION

One of the crucial problems in education today is student motivation. Of knowledge to be learned we possess a superabundance. Our pedagogical skills are reasonably well developed, and our physical resources plentiful. Nor are we without a good supply of students with intellectual competence. The crucial questions are: How insure that ability will be fully employed? How create a real hunger for learning? How encourage students to take initiative and responsibility for their own progress?

The problem is commonly approached in a dualistic fashion. "Motive" is regarded as an independent, separable force which can be treated as a thing-in-itself. Thus, "motivating students" is thought of after the analogy of a fueling operation. Something needs to be injected into students to energize them. Usually this is accomplished by verbal instruction, admonition, or exhortation. Parents put pressure on their children to achieve in school. Teachers lecture their pupils on the necessity for more effort. More recently the Russians have aided us in our campaign for motivation by the threat of surpassing us in production, thus adding to the other external compulsions the force of fear.

These dualistic approaches are futile because they provide an incorrect analysis of the problem. Motive, or will-to-learn, is not a thing-in-itself apart from persons and circumstances. It is an abstraction drawn from the concrete situation of persons striving to realize genuine purposes. Purposes arise naturally as human beings seek to relate themselves satisfyingly to the world presented to them. Why are Russian pupils on the whole more willing to work hard than American pupils? Primarily because the personal advantages obtained by successful academic performance are abundantly evident in Soviet society but not in American society. The American student who gets by with a minimum of effort may reap rewards of economic, political, or social advantage just as surely as the more eager student.

Poor student motivation is not a malady to be cured by direct means, as the dualist believes. It is a consequence of the disparity between academic assumptions and the realities of concrete social existence. If "the life of the mind" is to become an inspiring and energizing goal, as many who deplore the lack of academic motivation hope, it will not be accomplished through editorials or declamations, but only through the modification of culture and society in such a way that intellectual, artistic, and moral accomplishments are honored and rewarded not only in word but in actuality.

II. THE TREND TOWARD CONFORMITY

Many observers of the present educational scene are deeply troubled by the apparent trend of students toward conformity. The Jacob study of changing values in college is probably the most widely distributed expression of this concern. Teachers complain that students are submissive, conventional, and unquestioning. Gone are the healthy rebellion and scepticism of earlier generations of college students. Today's students, it is said, want answers, certainty, freedom from doubt.

In confronting this issue, the dualistic approach is still prevalent. Either students must be rebellious non-conformists, rugged individualists, or they must be organization people, other-directed adapters to the social environment. We must choose, it is said, between creativity and conformity, between independence and submergence in the mass. Beatnik non-conventionality is an example of electing the former alternative, as may also be true to some extent of extreme advocates of independent study and opponents of guidance counseling.

A non-dualistic analysis shows that we are not forced to choose between the independent individual and the social mass. Dewey correctly contrasted the old, *laissez-faire*, rugged individualism and the new socially responsible individualism. All human growth necessarily takes place within a social context. The individual cannot develop except by social interaction. And obviously no society can exist without constituent persons, who must conform to certain social agreements.

The proper question is not whether we shall choose to be individual or social, but what shall be the quality of the individual-social complex. Conformity is not bad in itself. Everything depends on what is conformed to and why. Few would object to students conforming to a pattern of rigorous critical inquiry or of enthusiasm for esthetic or moral excellence. The ideal community, as Dewey saw, is one in which there is the greatest possible mutually enriching interaction. In the democratic educative commonwealth, individual differences are respected and welcomed as strengthening and deepening the common experience, and the life of the group in turn empowers the individual and liberates him from the ineffectiveness and meaninglessness of isolation.

III. LIBERAL VS. PRACTICAL EDUCATION

The current educational debate not infrequently presupposes a clear opposition between liberal and practical education. Liberal studies are defined as those which are pursued for their own sake, while practical studies are instrumental to some further value. "Pure" knowledge is an end in itself; "applied" knowledge is a means to an end beyond itself. The contrast is clear in comparing liberal arts curricula with technical and professional courses, pure science with engineering, and the "fine arts" with the "useful" arts and crafts. Nowhere is the issue so sharply drawn as in the discussions of the liberal and technical elements in teacher education and in the debates between the proponents of the liberal arts colleges and of the schools of education for the preparation of teachers.

Little progress can be made in resolving this issue as long as the opposition implicit in the above analysis is presupposed. What is needed is a recognition of the continuity and interpenetration of the pure and the applied. Liberal studies can be true to their name only as they equip intelligence to fulfill goals deemed worthy of pursuit. Freedom is not a state of mind but a condition of activity, that is, of practice, broadly conceived. "Liberal" studies which effect no improvement in practice are non-liberating. The test of liberality is thus ultimately practical. Similarly, "practical" studies which do not rest upon an enlarged and enlivened intellectual grasp are to that extent practically deficient, for they lack the foundation for effective application to a variety of circumstances.

As recent studies by Earl McGrath and others have

shown, the development of higher education today is
bearing out the inseparability of the liberal and the
professional. So-called liberal arts colleges are becoming increasingly professional in orientation, as pressures
mount for education which can clearly be turned to
account in life work. At the same time, the professional schools are introducing more liberal arts work
into their curricula, to provide the breadth of outlook
and theoretical perspectives needed by practitioners
in a rapidly changing, complex, and precarious world.

IV. THE DECLINE IN MORALITY

Many today are concerned over what they believe is
a decline in morality, and they call for increased
emphasis on moral education. As in the issues discussed above, this problem is usually formulated
dualistically. Moral standards are conceived as having
an existence independent of the people who are judged
or guided by them. Morality is thus regarded as external to persons and situations, a quality of rightness
which needs to be put into people from the outside,
very much as in the case of motivation. The dualism
comes out further in the choice usually presented
between an absolute, objective morality and relative,
subjective standards of conduct (which can only by
courtesy be called moral). Morality is also confined
to a special domain of conduct, including sex behavior and observance of civil and criminal codes, while
other spheres of activity are not regarded as matters
of moral concern.

A non-dualistic view of morality recognizes the human and social context in which concepts of the
right are generated. Thus moral education is not the
imposition of ready-made standards but guidance in
the exercise of responsible and intelligent choice.
Morality is not absolute, because the context of con-

duct is ever changing. Neither is it purely relative, because there are regularities in personality and society. Morals are not objective only, because particular individuals and societies are inextricably involved in moral judgments, nor are they purely subjective, because standards are determined in relation to the given facts of the world as it is. Furthermore, moral concern covers all domains of human conduct. All free deliberate activity—all choice of better or worse—is matter for moral judgment.

Those who regard moral education from the non-dualistic standpoint will not so readily conclude that today's young people have lost moral fiber, simply because they do not adhere to the ways of their forefathers. Moral growth will be seen as the complex matter it is—as the development of the power to judge alternative modes of conduct in the light of the widest possible appraisal of consequences. Thus life will neither be guided by fixed traditional rules nor left to drift on the tide of convention or impulse. Direction will come from the funded experience of mankind, tested and improved by the agency of intelligence.

V. RELIGION IN EDUCATION

A widely discussed issue today is the place of religion in education. The debate usually proceeds between those who think religion should be included in education and those who think it should not, at least in public schools. In standard dualistic fashion, religion is conceived as something which can be injected into learning. Education either has religion or it has not. To "put religion" into the schools it is only necessary to say prayers, read from the Bible, have religious services, give courses in religion, establish religious groups, and so forth. Without such things education is secular.

When they are included, the sacred element has been provided for. To the natural learnings the religious acts add a supernatural complement.

As against this way of defining the problem, a unitive approach affirms the possibility of finding the religious *within* the so-called secular processes. Dewey made a distinction between "religions"—institutional and creedal forms of commitment—and the "religious" dimension or aspect in experience, referring to the outreach toward infinitely profound and inclusive ideality. A somewhat similar idea is expressed in Tillich's concept of religion as "ultimate concern."

The problems of religion in education—at least in the public schools—can be satisfactorily approached only when religion is understood as an interpretation of human experience, in continuity with other modes of interpretation, and when the teaching of religion is conducted in such a way as to enrich and unite rather than impoverish and divide the educational community. These ends can be realized only so long as religion is primarily conceived as having its source and justification in relationship to the problems of men trying to find meaning and sustenance in the world surrounding them.

In the above discussion I have emphasized only one aspect of Dewey's teaching. Many other philosophers have fought dualism, in ways quite different from Dewey's. From this we may rightly infer that the war on dualism is not the unique and distinctive feature of Dewey's philosophy. Nevertheless, it is for him a fundamental theme, and one which enables us to see his thought at work over a wide range of problems.

Dualism is perennially appealing because it seems to give clear and definite answers. Amid the inevitable perplexities of life, we are tempted to over-simplify the issues by resort to exclusive classifications. But

refuge in the black and white, either-or type of thinking is as perilous as it is easy. John Dewey called us
out of these confusions and delusions to a discipline
of unitive thought which is both more rigorous in its
demands and more faithful to the truth we aim to
serve.

RELEVANT READING

Dewey, John, "Dualism," in Paul Monroe, ed., *A Cyclopedia of Education*," Vol. II. New York: The Macmillan Company, 1911.

—— *Democracy and Education*. New York: The Macmillan Company, 1916.

—— "Duality and Dualism." *Journal of Philosophy*, XIV (August 30, 1917).

—— *Theory of Valuation*. International Encyclopedia of Unified Science, Vol. II, Foundations of the Unity of Science, No. 4. Chicago: The University of Chicago Press, 1939.

Phenix, Philip H., *Philosophy of Education*. New York: Henry Holt & Company, Inc., 1958.

—— *Realms of Meaning*. New York: McGraw-Hill Book Company, Inc., 1964.

Schilpp, Paul A., ed., *The Philosophy of John Dewey*. The Library of Living Philosophers, Vol. I. Evanston and Chicago: Northwestern University, 1939.

Sheldon, Wilmon H., "The Conquest of Dualism." *New Republic*, CXXI (October 17, 1949).

The Vain Quest for Unity

JOHN DEWEY'S SOCIAL AND EDUCATIONAL THOUGHT
IN RETROSPECT

❧

Frederic Lilge

In current discussions of the crisis in American education, the name of John Dewey has become perhaps
more widely familiar than it was during his lifetime.
Whereas he was then the symbol of all that was good
and progressive to a great part of the American educational profession, his value has now been reversed. He
is vaguely associated in the minds of a large public
with the authorship of all that is wrong with the
schools. Even though criticisms may be directed to
widely different and not necessarily related aspects of
public education, they often assume that there must
be a central source from which all the evil sprang.
It is true that Dewey had his most ardent disciples in
the teachers colleges, and that through them his influence reached down to the teachers in the elementary
grades. But the shape or deformity of the schools is
the result of multiple forces that act upon them. Not
only contemporary philosophy but psychology, not
only academic theories but popular fashions and the
general temper of the age leave their marks upon them.
Very likely the protest against authority during the
jazz and prohibition era, the "fun morality" and the

This selection originally appeared in the *Proceedings of the Philosophy of Education Society,* 1959. Mr. Lilge is Professor of Education at the University of California.

general bewilderment of modern society have determined educational practice more profoundly than any single pedagogical theory. Those influences are pervasive and impossible to measure precisely, and so it is easier to put the blame on the writings of Dewey and his disciples.

Another kind of critique, less questionable and more promising, is possible. Instead of condemning Dewey's philosophy by the malpractices imputed to it, its main ideas and assumptions may be subjected to critical analysis on a broad theoretical plane. Without becoming involved in a technical discussion of Dewey's metaphysics or his logic, this essay will proceed directly to the ultimate concern that holds together his large and many-sided work, the unification of contemporary culture for the sake of a common, more closely shared democratic life. His two main interests, philosophy and education, received their meaning by subserving the paramount purpose of social reform—philosophy, by furnishing a general diagnosis of what Dewey regarded as a prolonged and serious cultural crisis; education, by becoming the chief and perhaps the only means of solving the problems which constituted that crisis. His quest for unity and commonality will be the general concern of this essay. It will seek to discover whether his diagnosis is still relevant to the present, and, if it is not, how adequate it was in the first place. The answer to these questions bears directly upon the current discussions of the aims and problems of American education. For if his diagnosis of the cultural situation should have lost much of its relevance, the same fate must also have befallen his educational ideas which were formed largely, though not entirely, in response to it. In that case it becomes clear that mere tinkering with the present educational machinery to fit it for some supposed emergency will never do. Instead we shall have to reconsider the very meaning of education, and this is possible only by relating it to the human situation of today.

Although statements on cultural crisis are scattered through many of Dewey's writings, they became concentrated and urgent during the decade between the beginning of the Great Depression and World War II. Long critical of a business culture that shirked its social responsibilities, Dewey concluded that it was necessary in the cultural and economic sphere to go forward from liberalism. During the adverse economic conditions of the thirties and the rise of West-European totalitarianism, many people came to share his belief. But the way out of social irresponsibility and conflict and the attainment of a society beyond "enlightened self-interest" and the profit system led in different directions for different persons. For many troubled Western intellectuals it led through the Finland station. For others who regarded the reform of social institutions as less important than an inner conversion of individuals, recovery was possible only through a replenishment of life at its religious sources. This, for example, was the view Toynbee expressed in the latter volumes of his *Study of History*.

Dewey, who accepted neither Marxism-Leninism nor a new universal religion, developed a faith of his own that yet contained some elements of both gospels of salvation. Like the Marxists, he regarded the transformability of social institutions by rational means as of primary importance. At the same time, he invested these means, which he called the scientific method and the method of intelligence, with a quasi-religious significance. The source of these effective and mystic overtones of Dewey's instrumentalism lay, I think, in a deep longing for unity and commonality, a longing which was denied satisfaction by such diverse systems as economic liberalism on the one hand and by dogmatic religion on the other.

Dewey has commonly been celebrated for his projection of a democratic school that would be the cradle of a new society redeemed from conflict and from all divisive institutions. Yet, his conception of democracy was clouded by ambivalence that prevented him from promoting the unity he desired. He adhered in part to the instrumental or operational definition of democracy, according to which men agree on methods and means to secure social cohesion but leave the ends of life uninvolved. His conception of a democratic education as an exercise in practical intelligence and co-operative action accords with this view of democracy. However, the diversity of basic values and the conflict of beliefs which this purely instrumental conception allows were bound to deny the spiritual unity and the common faith he longed for.

If democracy was to become fully effective as a united human endeavor, agreement had to be extended from methods and instrumentalities to a set of values and ends. Dewey proposed the philosophy of naturalism because it promised to liberate man from all supranatural authorities. By thus giving man his freedom, it put the control of social institutions and practices into his hands and directed his energies and interests to the solution of his social problems. Obviously, this identification of democracy with naturalism led to a deprecation of the social value of other philosophies. "Democracy cannot obtain adequate recognition of its own meaning or coherent practical realization as long as anti-naturalism operates to delay and frustrate the use of methods by which alone understanding and consequent ability to guide social relationships are attained."[1] Anti-naturalism was a broad epithet and, although it seemed to be directed chiefly against the

---

[1] John Dewey, "Anti-naturalism in Extremis," in *Naturalism and the Human Spirit,* Y. H. Krikorian, ed. (New York: Columbia University Press, 1944), p. 3.

philosophy of the Catholic Church, it covered any
philosophic view that gave prominence in human life
to powers and claims which man neither created nor
controlled. In the polemics that inevitably ensued and
that make up much of American educational philosophy over the last quarter century, the followers of
Dewey frequently implied that anti-naturalists were
either insincere or ineffectual supporters of the democratic way of life. The futility of this polemic and the
injustice of the charge would have been apparent from
the beginning, had the conception of democracy been
limited to its commonly accepted instrumental meaning. To accuse those who do not share his particular
philosophic beliefs of delaying and frustrating the solution of social problems obviously did not promote the
unity Dewey had set out to achieve.

The aspirations for spiritual unity and a common
faith were not always made dependent upon the acceptance of a scientific naturalism. From the fragments
of Dewey's autobiographical writing, it appears that
they were deeply rooted in his personal experience. He
spoke of discontinuities and separations that lacerated
him: for example, the separation of pleasure and duty,
the self and the world, man and nature which may have
formed part of his New England heritage. When at
Johns Hopkins University he came under the influence
of Hegelianism, he seems to have felt great relief at
learning that there were philosophies which admitted
no discontinuities and which in fact held out the
promise of a final unification of cultural life. This Hegelian promise left a lasting impression on Dewey's
mind even though he eventually rejected Hegel's metaphysics. In order to realize the promise within his own
philosophy, Dewey had to delegate the work of Hegel's
superhuman mind, in which all contradictions and
absurdities became spiritually sublimated, to the human
intelligence: *it* was to resolve the conflicts and chaos

into some kind of order within which man could become secure and have a dignified existence. Dewey was aware that this meant arduous and incessant labor. To inspire men with confidence in its eventual outcome and to banish the myth of Sisyphus from the contemporary mind required a total commitment of men's energies to the tasks before them. This moral strenuousness was, I believe, the cause of Dewey's deprecation of philosophies that neither shared his optimism nor involved man wholly in the work of social amelioration.

A recurrent theme in Dewey's thought indicative of his quest for unity is his condemnation of the separation of science and morals. He believed that this separation lay at the root of the cultural crisis, and that to destroy it was one of the chief burdens of education. Young people should be shown that moral beliefs are not intrinsically true, but that they arise under certain conditions and have observable consequences when acted upon. In the light of these consequences our moral beliefs should be subject to revision, much as our ideas about physical reality are. In a recent book, *The Ideal and the Community* by I. B. Berkson, this analogy between moral action and scientific experiment has been subjected to critical examination. Important differences exist between the two, but they do not produce the fatally divisive power which Dewey attributed to them. The adequacy of Dewey's diagnosis of cultural crisis is thereby called into question.

The single-mindedness of the social reformer is well illustrated by Dewey's polemical reviews of the history of European philosophy in *The Quest for Certainty* and in *Reconstruction in Philosophy*. Since the main obstacles to the extension of the experimental method lay in certain religious and philosophical traditions, it was necessary to subject these traditions to criticism. The logical or internal difficulties of philosophies

interested him less than what he judged to be their im-
moral implications. It would be untrue to say that
Dewey attached no value to historical continuities. He
spoke of philosophies, for example, as attempts to "define the larger patterns of continuity which are woven
in affecting the enduring junctions of a stubborn past
and an insistent future." But the overall impression left
by these two works is that the prejudices of the past
intrude into the present so as to prevent the living from
posing their questions in adequate and relevant terms.
Dewey's scorn was mainly directed at the so-called
classical tradition in philosophy that symbolized for
him an escape from the vicissitudes of existence. "If
contemporary Western man were completely deprived
of all the old basic notions about knowledge and action,
he would assume, with a fair degree of confidence,
that it lies within his power to achieve a reasonable
degree of security in life."[2] In short, it was morally
justifiable to break with traditions if they disparaged
action and change and extolled contemplation and
permanence. Without such a break modern man would
be unable to realize his potentialities.

The plea to cast off burdensome traditions had educational repercussions. If education were to consist
largely in learning to solve present problems, history
could be admitted into the curriculum only on condition that it helped in the understanding and solution
of such problems. Dewey saw no difficulties here, for
in his view history was inescapably the history of the
present. Not only that, it was also the history of what
is contemporaneously judged to be important in the
present. Historical inquiry, in his view, was controlled
by the dominant problems and conceptions of the culture of the period in which it was written.

Whether all historiography is culturally determined

[2] John Dewey, *The Quest for Certainty* (New York: Putnam,
1930), p. 13.

by the major problems of the present is a question properly to be answered by ascertaining how historians have in fact selected the past events and experiences with which they concern themselves. The answer is not likely to support Dewey's assertions. One thinks of Gibbon, for instance, as he "sat musing amidst the ruins of the Capitol" and of the desire that arose in him to know how the greatness of Rome perished. Or to mention a contemporary example, there is Lovejoy whose study in the history of an idea, *The Great Chain of Being*, goes back to his being puzzled by some obscure reference to it in Pope's *Essay on Man*. The fact is that the historian's interest is not usually identical with that of the social reformer. The latter looks to history for such aid as it may give to determine a program of social action, and he singles out for attention those ideas, achievements, and interests whose development and confirmation he desires. Dewey himself selected the economic, industrial, and scientific aspects of history as deserving chief attention because they illustrate man's progress in adapting natural forces to social uses, and it was for this that Dewey wanted history taught in the schools.

The historian, on the other hand, is likely to be interested in the past for its own sake, and he accepts this interest as self-justifying. The break with traditions that were regarded as anti-naturalistic, anti-scientific, and therefore anti-democratic became the battle cry of many of Dewey's sympathizers who turned his social and educational philosophy into an evangel. Boyd Bode, to cite only one example, wrote that "the issue of democracy versus tradition . . . must be made the central concern of the democratic school."[3] He called Platonism "one of the major tragedies of human civilization," and he attacked the Harvard Re-

[3] Boyd Bode, *Progressive Education at the Crossroads* (New York: Newson, 1938), p. 71.

port on *General Education in a Free Society* because it
was sympathetic to the cultural heritage of the West
and recommended it as the basis of a liberal education,
instead of exposing what he called its spirit of "two-
worldism." Dewey himself was more balanced in his
views and more knowledgeable of the traditions he
criticized. Yet he too feared that democracy and a
democratic education were threatened by moral and
religious traditions that comprise the achievements of
science because they had originated before the modern
scientific age. Democracy implied for him the acceptance of a philosophy of scientific naturalism. Beyond
this it required an emotional commitment and a quasi-
religious faith. A conception of democracy so expanded beyond what was previously called the instrumental definition was bound to come into conflict with
other beliefs, religious or secular, that did not place
supreme importance on man's political and social life.
It is necessary to elaborate on this quasi-religious valuation of democracy and on Dewey's consequent search
for an exemplification of the model society he had in
mind.

The distinctive trait of democratic education, according to Dewey, was that it led the individual to
participate in, and to identify himself with, "conjoint
communicated experience." Shared experience and
communication were for him not only means but
ends, not only instrumental but also intrinsic goods.
Thus, communication is transmitted into communion,
and the experience of sharing radiates a warmth of be-
longing that purely rational agreements concerning the
rules of democratic life cannot produce. "When the
emotional force, the mystic force one might say, of the
miracles of the shared life and shared experience is
spontaneously felt, the hardness and crudeness of contemporary life will be bathed in a light that never was

on land or sea."[4] In such passages Dewey spoke no longer as the advocate of critical intelligence, but as a social visionary who looked to a society of the future redeemed of conflicts and aglow with the happiness of common ends and enjoyments.

He realized that serious obstacles lay in the way of that redemption and happiness, and he devoted himself to removing these rather than to elaborating his social vision, a significant difference as compared with Marx. Capitalism, for example, imposed upon men competitive and acquisitive habits that isolated them from one another. The old tradition of political liberalism insisted that negative freedom, freedom from restraint and compulsion, was all that society should guarantee. Religious and philosophical traditions, finally, by encouraging the inner life or a trust in transcendent realities, provided spiritual reserves that precluded any need for the "miracle of shared life." Apart from rather vague occasional suggestions for political action, Dewey relied on re-education to break the power of these traditions.

There was a time when Dewey believed that the ideal society conceived as a spiritual community unified by common ends was being realized in the Soviet Union. After his visit to Russia in 1928, he wrote that he found there "a widespread and moving religious quality" which infected intellectuals and the common people alike. Soviet intellectuals, he remarked, "have a task that is total and constructive. They are organic members of an organic going movement." The Soviet teaching profession seemed to him endowed with dignity because it was taken into confidence by the government and acted as a partner in the great enterprise of social and economic planning. The work of the

[4] John Dewey, *Reconstruction in Philosophy* (New York: Holt, 1920), p. 211.

schools was meaningful because it helped to create a new man and a social faith. Dewey was not blind even then to the threats to liberty and truth in Soviet society. But his critical powers relaxed when he was confronted by what he took to be the common aspirations of the people and the apparent faith in their own power to remake themselves and their society. Soviet socialism was at that time nearing the end of its theorizing, idealistic phase; the brutal realities of collectivization and the purges lay still ahead. It was, therefore, tempting to see in Soviet socialism an epiphany of the society one longed for, especially when Russia was contrasted with America on the brink of the great economic depression. Not that Dewey wished Soviet institutions or ideology transferred to American society. Still he could not help admiring Soviet socialism because it did not seem to suffer from the conflicts and problems inherent in capitalist liberal society. In comparison with Soviet schools, American schools appeared to him "dull and dispirited" because they were not committed to a great cause and the curriculum was not unified by a common social program. American intellectuals functioned only as social critics, instead of becoming participants in social reconstruction. Similar conclusions were reached by other visitors to the Soviet Union at that time—George S. Counts, for example—and found wide adoption among socially progressive educators.

The admiration for Soviet socialism proved a passing phase in Dewey's thought, and it is mentioned here for its intellectual rather than for any political significance. He appeared to project in it his desire for a society in which the spiritual communion of all would dissolve the "hardness" and "crudeness" that seemed to be a part of liberal society, not only in its then current inglorious phase but permanently. It is easier today than it was thirty years ago to realize how deeply de-

pendent on the Marxian model of social thought
American educators and intellectuals became. Precisely
because they were preoccupied with the phenomena of
social disintegration in general and with the weaknesses
of democracy in particular, a unified society, harmonious and conflictless, appeared to them to solve not only
social but educational problems as well. "If we could
establish a social program in the manner of Russia,"
wrote Boyd Bode, "our educational problems would
largely disappear."[5] Dewey and his disciples realized,
of course, that this could not be done; their democratic
loyalties restrained them. But they did not examine the
dilemma into which their aspirations had led them. If
the apotheosis of democracy depended upon means
which their respect for liberty and truth forbade them
to adopt, their ideal was left standing high and dry.
For pragmatists who taught that means were continuous with ends, this was especially perplexing, and it
should have caused them to question the validity of
their social ideal.

There could be only two exits from the dilemma.
One was to retain the belief in democracy as a quasi-
religious community and to seek its realization by un-
reprehensible and generally approved methods. Yet
such methods as compromise, negotiation, debate, due
process of law, and the like limited democracy to the
instrumental meaning described above; they were unable to achieve the more inclusive unity that was desired. The other solution was to abandon the apotheosis
of democracy and to be content with a more rational
and functional conception, such as David Riesman defines as "conditional co-operation towards specific
short-term goals." This implies a rejection of all ecstatic
and utopian forms of association, in an acknowledg-
ment that men do not fully realize themselves through

[5] W. H. Kilpatrick, ed., *The Educational Frontier* (New York:
The Century Co., 1933), p. 23.

participation in programs of social action. Neither
Dewey nor his educational disciples found the logic
of these alternatives to their liking, and as a result they
bequeathed to American institutions of professional
education a vague, muddle-headed idealism. Although
this tradition has greatly diminished in recent years,
where it lingers public education is regarded as a crusade or a cause that requires missionary zeal from its
believers and a united front against all non-believers.
This partisan spirit, which many professional educationists have mistaken for a philosophy of education,
is one of the reasons for the well-known alienation of
departments of education from the rest of the university.

In the quarter-century that has passed since those
ideas were in vogue, marked changes have taken place
in the social conditions and in the intellectual climate
of this country. The particular economic problems of
the thirties to which Dewey and his followers re-
sponded are no longer in the center of attention. The
reason is not that they were solved by the socialist reconstruction recommended by the philosophers, but
that rapid technological progress, greatly stimulated by
the last war, and an expanding although not basically
revised economy have provided rising incomes and
continued upward social mobility. As for inflation,
automation, and other problems of today, few people
look to a socialized economy for their solution. In the
political sphere, the effect of Stalinism on many Western intellectuals was a disillusionment not only with
Soviet socialism but with leftist ideologies in general.
Many discovered that democratic society, whatever its
imperfections, proved more viable than they had believed. The traditions and institutions which Dewey
had regarded as weakening and frustrating the realization of a democratic society continue to exist without
causing the same anxiety. The values and ends of life

give no more evidence than before of being derived from or justified by science; and people continue to differ about them without thereby endangering the cohesion of society. The identification of democracy with the philosophy of a militant, scientific naturalism has not become more widely accepted. On the contrary, non-naturalistic philosophies continue to be held by many members of the American educational profession. Finally, Dewey's vision of democracy as a spiritual community, unified by a quasi-religious faith and by a commitment to an inclusive program of social action, elicits little response today.

However cursory and incomplete this survey of the contemporary social and educational situation may be, it is difficult to escape the conclusion that Dewey's diagnosis of cultural crisis has lost its relevance. Such causes of it as he identified continue to operate without resulting in the disintegration he feared; and, conversely, the remedies he proposed for its resolution have not been applied, without society being greatly the worse for that. It is of course true that American democracy remains imperfect and contains many conflicts. There are different ways of accounting for, and estimating the gravity of, these imperfections. The Christian, for example, regards them as inevitable because for him all human institutions and actions are infected with sin. A pessimistic naturalist like Santayana believed that a thousand reforms and revolutions have left the world at bottom as corrupt as ever. They may both be right; the history of the twentieth century certainly furnished little proof to the contrary.

The ultimate interpretations are here left aside, however, in favor of a more limited contextual one. I would argue that the enduring conflicts and tensions of democratic society (in which I do not include such problems as interracial strife) appear grave and even fatal when they are viewed in the utopian perspective, that

is, when the attainment of a rational and harmonious
society is believed to be a possibility, whether by the
mystiques of communication and the scientific method
as in Dewey, or by the historical dialectic as in Marx.
Once this perspective of utopia is abandoned, a more
realistic understanding of the processes and mecha-
nisms by which democratic society is maintained re-
asserts itself. Thus American political science and
sociology, formerly preoccupied with the forces of
social disintegration, are now interested in the processes of social integration. Many social scientists pres-
ently concern themselves, for example, with the balances a viable democratic society must sustain between
cleavage and consensus, competition and co-operation,
majority power and minority rights, and other conflicting forces. Utopian social thought, and Marxism in
particular, paid no attention to these balances because
they recognized only two social states, that of absolute
conflict which is self-destructive, and that of absolute
harmony which presumably does not require the mech-
anisms by which democratic society settles opposing
claims and achieves a reasonable measure of unity.
Although Dewey was not a Marxist, his longing for
unity made him susceptible to the influences of utopian
social thought. This influence did not extend to specific doctrines; it was limited to a strong emotional
appeal. The possibility of seeing democratic society redeemed from conflicts captured his imagination and
that of many socially progressive educators. In fact,
it seemed to become for them a substitute for religious
hope.

   In the final analysis, the loss of relevance of Dewey's
social and educational thought can be explained not
only by the fact that the times have changed, but also
by a basic inadequacy of his philosophy. In his desire
to resolve all conflicts into a higher unity, he slighted
certain realities. His view of the relation of the indi-

vidual to society may serve as illustration. He regarded social efficiency and personal culture as identical because he believed that, as a result of an appropriate education, the intellectual and creative life of an individual would merge with his social functions, services, and duties. When the whole of society was reformed as a result of the re-education of its members, the worth of an individual could be measured in terms of his participation in common activities. Dewey did not project a brave new world composed of automata. He granted the uniqueness of individuals and appreciated their contributions to the common life. But he denied that there was a life of the spirit and a happiness apart from sharing common activities. Spiritual culture in the quietistic sense he condemned as futile and as having "something rotten about it." "What is called inner," he declared, "is simply that which does not connect with others—which is not capable of free and full communication."[6] He was aware, of course, that many men continued to separate social duty from individual excellence, but he regarded this as a remnant of a bankrupt culture. The new education would replace that division by "the power to join freely and fully in shared activities."

There are two objections to this identification of the inner with the public life of individuals. One is that Dewey dwelt upon the ideal aspects of group experience with little relation to the actual ways in which the business of society gets done. Communication and sharing belong to the vocabulary of education and religion rather than to that of politics and economics. In spite of his avowed pragmatism, Dewey was captivated by the democratic process and its ideal possibilities, and this dims his social philosophy with an air of unreality. Under ordinary circumstances the life of the individual

[6] John Dewey, *Democracy and Education* (New York: Macmillan, 1916), p. 143.

is not wholly absorbed in group experiences. In societies that lay some claim to a civilized life, such experiences are balanced by the individual's desire to live in a world of his own, both real and imaginative. This balance is upset in times of upheaval and emergency such as revolution and war when group experiences swell to a high pitch of excitement and common effort becomes capable of powerful social action. As already observed, Dewey was impressed by the popular enthusiasm aroused by the Russian revolution, and he was similarly inclined to believe in the creative potential of war. In 1917 he favored America's entry into the war because it might become an instrument for realizing a new international order and thus be "a war of compelling moral import." One of his former students, Randolph Bourne, disagreed sharply.[7] If war had been too much for the liberal to prevent, how could he hope to control it? Dewey deluded himself, he wrote, if he believed he could prevent the crude passions, the bigotry and the suppression of civil liberties which accompanied America's entry into the war. Instrumentalist philosophy, he remarked, had never confronted the inexorable and the irrational; it was so haunted by optimism that it tried to turn even war into a tool of creative intelligence.

His criticisms pointed to the limitations of Dewey's philosophy. Though fearful of the futility and rottenness of the secluded inner life, Dewey seemed unaware that the same faults might pervade the public life. To him the goodness of free and full communication, the happiness of the shared life were self-evident. He regarded these processes as inherently rational and could not conceive of the possibility that democratic society, too, could be deluded.

[7] Dewey's essays on war are contained in *Character and Events,* Vol. 2 (New York: Holt, 1929). For R. Bourne's critique, see his *Untimely Papers* (New York: B. W. Huebsch, 1919).

From this the second objection follows directly. In the history of Western education the humanities, and to a lesser degree the fine arts, have been regarded as the traditional means by which the life of the spirit and individual excellence may be fostered. The more philosophic-minded among the humanists, Montaigne for example, justified these values on the ground that an individual requires a life apart from the noise and movements of the world for the sake of his emotional sanity and intellectual integrity. Dewey, to whom the sanctity of the spiritual life was suspect, was unable to grasp this meaning or to subscribe to this justification of the humanities. It is true that his book *Art As Experience* affirmed the existence of consummatory experiences as compared with instrumental goods. Yet this recognition scarcely affected his educational theory, which remained strenuously moralist, reformist, and socialist. Philosophy and history he approved as subjects of instruction on condition that they prove themselves useful instruments of social diagnosis and social progress. His treatment of literature was similar.

Although Dewey frequently stated the importance of developing individual capacities, he neglected to concern himself with the question of how the teaching of literature may be said to aid in its growth. His main work on educational theory, *Democracy and Education*, contains chapters on the teaching of such subjects as science, geography, and history, and it shows how these can be turned into means of "socializing intelligence." The scant attention given to the teaching of literature was intended as warning rather than encouragement. Dewey was almost entirely concerned to show that humanistic studies had dominated the curriculum in the past because men sought authority in literature, sacred and profane, instead of in nature. He described Western Europe and America down to the end of the nineteenth century as living on a culture

borrowed from ancient Greece. Instruction was based
on ready-made ideas rather than on independent inquiry. Furthermore, he said literary studies were aristo-
cratic, characteristic of a leisured class that scorned
economic and technical interests as beneath its dignity.
This historical commentary on the use and associations
of literature was not calculated to encourage its study
for its own sake or for esthetic reasons. Rather it ques-
tioned the value of literature to a democratic education
unless the subject could be integrated with the social
studies—as, in fact, it frequently has been—so as to
contribute to an understanding of the dominant problems of contemporary society.

Whatever the validity of Dewey's historical judgments, they are really irrelevant to the educational
problem that is involved. The fact that literature may
once have been put to anti-scientific and undemocratic
uses does not answer the question of what its intrinsic
values are and what part they should play in a young
person's education. Dewey never asked this question
apparently because he did not think it important.
Humanism for him meant a social humanism that
would teach young people to take an intelligent interest in such problems as poverty, insanity, city
planning, and the conservation of natural resources.
Although there is merit in this, it neglects to help
young people discover and perfect their own humanity. As preparation for life today, this appears as a
serious failure. In a society whose growing affluence
is not matched by a clearer sense of values, it would
seem that education should help individuals to find
their own vital center. Civilization is not all a matter
of an indefinite future, it must also be exemplified in
the present by what persons themselves are. There is
no more reason today than there was in the past for
believing that the evils of organized social life can be
exterminated if only all educative efforts are bent in

that direction. Once this is admitted, the socialization of the individual will cease to be acceptable as the over-all aim of education.

RELEVANT READING

Childs, John L., "Cultural Factors in Dewey's Philosophy of Education." *Teachers College Record*, LI (December, 1949).

Dewey, John, *The School and Society*, Revised. Chicago: The University of Chicago Press, 1915.

—— *Human Nature and Conduct: an Introduction to Social Psychology*. New York: The Modern Library, 1930.

—— "American Education and Culture." *New Republic*, VII (July 1, 1916).

—— *Impressions of Soviet Russia and the Revolutionary World, Mexico–China–Turkey*. New York: New Republic, Inc., 1929.

—— *Characters and Events*. Joseph Ratner, ed. New York: Henry Holt and Company, Inc., 1929.

—— "Education and Our Present Social Problems." *School and Society*, XXXVII (April 15, 1933).

—— "Education for a Changing Social Order." *Addresses and Proceedings*, National Education Association, 1934.

—— "Class Struggle and the Democratic Way." *Social Frontier*, II (May, 1936).

Lilge, Frederic, "John Dewey, 1859–1959: Reflections on His Educational and Social Thought." *Educational Forum*, XXIV (March, 1960).

—— "John Dewey in Retrospect: An American Reconsideration." *British Journal of Educational Studies*, VIII (May, 1960).

Meiklejohn, Alexander, *Education Between Two Worlds*. New York: Harper and Brothers, 1942.

White, Morton G., *Social Thought in America: The Revolt against Formalism*. New York: Viking Press, Inc., 1949.

Philosophy and Education

❀

Knowledge and Intelligence

❧

Alexander Meiklejohn

We turn now from the war cries of pragmatism to its problems and theories. As we do so it is important to note how closely connected is Dewey's study of education with his study of philosophy. In his great book, *Democracy and Education*, Dewey says, "Philosophy is the theory of education as a deliberately conducted enterprise."[1] Again, "Philosophy may even be defined as the general theory of education."[2] And still again, "The most penetrating definition of philosophy which can be given, then, is that it is the theory of education in its more general phases."[3] And, finally, "Education is the laboratory in which philosophic distinctions become concrete and are tested."[4] It is clear that we shall not know Dewey's theory of education unless we know what his philosophy is.

Now the central problem of Dewey's philosophy is the central problem of every student of teaching. It has to do with the relation between theory and practice, between facts and values, between knowledge and intelligence. Every school which relies upon words and symbols is trying to use knowing in such a way as to

This selection appeared originally as a chapter in *Education Between Two Worlds*, 1942 (Copyright 1942 by Harper and Brothers). Professor Meiklejohn, emeritus President of Amherst College, died in 1965.

[1] John Dewey, *Democracy and Education* (New York: Macmillan, 1922), p. 387.

[2] *Ibid.*, p. 388.

[3] *Ibid.*, p. 386.

[4] *Ibid.*, p. 384.

make behavior more intelligent. These two are not identical. A man may "know" without "being wise." He may be wise without having much formalized knowledge. A chemist, for example, may be learned about the behavior of gases, and may yet be foolish about the use of gases in warfare. Intellectual skill is not identical with practical efficiency. And yet knowledge can be useful. It can contribute to intelligence. To make it do so is the primary business of the school. To understand how it does so is the primary business of educational theory.

The problem which arises as we relate theory to practice is familiar but elusive. If, for example, we are studying the housing conditions of a great city the search for knowledge will reveal, in detail, the fact of social inequality. Some families are lavishly supplied with rooms and equipment. Other families are living in conditions which are, as we say, "unfit for human habitation." Our procedures of investigation will make that information exact, complete, and orderly. But, then, another question arises. It is a question, not of facts, but of values. Is it wrong or undesirable that there should be such inequality of living standards? Should action be taken to change the situation? Our knowledge of the facts alone does not answer that question. It merely provides usable information. But the question itself arises from our conviction of the relative merits of equality and inequality. If I believe that such inequality is evil, then that belief becomes a ground for action. If I have no such judgments of value then action would be meaningless. In a word, intelligence needs not only knowledge of facts but also principles of judgment. And the question as to the relation between theory and practice is "Where do these value principles come from? On what basis are they founded?" That question is primary for any theory of society or any theory of education.

I

Now Dewey's clearest statement of the relation between facts and values, between theory and practice, between knowledge and intelligence is given when he draws the distinction between the sciences and philosophy. The sciences are, for him, the culmination of the human striving for knowledge. Philosophy, on the other hand, is our most deliberate and systematic attempt at wisdom. "Inquiry" seeks to discover what the world is and does. "Reflection" tries to assess the values of life, to determine what men should be and do. These two intellectual enterprises represent the attempt to "know" and the attempt to "be wise" at their most highly conscious levels. If we can see how they differ, how they are related, how they work together in the lives of men, we shall have Dewey's account of what is, for the teacher, the most significant aspect of human behavior. We shall have at once his "philosophy" and his "general theory of education."

II

The most striking defect in Dewey's "general theory of education" is its disparagement of intelligence. He does not deny the importance of "wisdom" which is "based in knowledge." On the contrary no one has insisted more eagerly, more vigorously than he, that knowledge shall be intelligently used in the guidance of human behavior. But he does cast doubt upon the "objective validity" of that procedure. In what may be called his "subjective" mood he draws the sharpest of contrasts between the scientific and the practical activities of mankind. The findings of the sciences are tested and verified. They are warranted by evidence. But the judgments of wisdom, the choices of value, have no such warrant in evidence. They are untested, unverified, unwarranted. And, that being true, the whole structure of education which rests upon them, is likewise lacking in support. It is equally true, however, that Dewey has another, an objective mood, in which judgments of value are said to be criticized, tested and evaluated. Both these moods are present throughout his thinking. In fact his intellectual career is largely one of conflict between them. But that conflict is never resolved. As we attempt to follow his thinking about society and education, the course of that struggle is, of necessity, the dominant motive of our discussion.

III

In *Democracy and Education* Dewey formulates the problem of which we are speaking. And he deals with it chiefly in his subjective mood. All knowledge, he tells us, comes from the sciences. "Knowledge, grounded knowledge, is science; it represents objects which have been settled, ordered, disposed of rationally."[5] All knowing, it would seem, is obtained by the sciences. In so far as they have finished their work there is no more "knowing" to be done. What then does philosophy do? If the philosopher does not add to the stock of human knowledge about men and the world, what is his business?

In the twenty-fourth chapter of *Democracy and Education*, which deals with the philosophy of education, Dewey's answer to this question is explicit, if not altogether clear. "It is for the sciences," he tells us, "to say what generalisations are tenable about the world and what they specifically are. But when we ask what sort of permanent disposition of action toward the world the scientific disclosures exact of us we are

5 Dewey, *op. cit.,* p. 380.

raising a philosophic question."[6] Philosophy, he seems
to say, does not tell what men are nor what the world
is. It tells what men should do with their world. It
seeks for principles of behavior. Those principles, it
appears, are not "known." How then are they acquired? On what basis are they held or discarded?
How are they justified or repudiated? What does
"exact of us" mean as describing the procedure by
which philosophic action goes beyond scientific
knowledge?

The answer to that question is given, in the chapter
on the philosophy of education, where Dewey reviews
his argument as a whole. He has advanced, he tells us
by three steps. First, there is an account of "the general
features of education as the process by which social
groups maintain their continuous existence."[7] This
general study takes "no specific account" of "the *kind*
of society aiming at its own perpetuation through education."[8] The second step describes democracy and
aristocracy as opposing "kinds" of society. It also
adopts democracy as its program, rejects aristocracy,
and analyzes teaching on that basis. The third step
considers the "present limitations" of the "actual real-
isation" of the enterprise.

Now, in the progress of this threefold argument, it
is the second step which is taken by philosophy. When
democracy and aristocracy have been set face to face
as opposing social programs either of which education
might serve, a choice is made between them. That
choice is not made by any science nor by any combina-
tion of sciences. It is made by philosophy. Dewey, as a
philosopher, has adopted "a permanent disposition of
action toward the world." He is a democrat.

6 *Ibid.*, p. 379.
7 *Ibid.*, p. 375.
8 *Ibid.*, p. 375.

But how is the choice made? Is it justified by evidence? Is it "grounded" like the conclusions of science?
We could answer that question if we could understand the phrase "exact of us," in the passage already
quoted. That phrase suggests that the values come out
of the facts, are "exacted" by them. But the suggestion
is not there clarified. Dewey does, however, tell us, in
another statement how principles of values are chosen.
They are "taken for granted." In describing the second, philosophic, step in his argument he says, "The
sort of education appropriate to the development of a
democratic community was then explicitly taken as
the criterion of the further, more detailed analysis of
education."[9] And again, "Save for incidental criticisms
designed to illustrate principles by force of contrast,
this (philosophic) phase of the discussion *took for
granted* the democratic criterion and its application in
present social life."[10]

Here then, so far as the argument of *Democracy and
Education* goes, is Dewey's separation of science and
philosophy, of knowledge and intelligence. The sciences have to do with knowledge of objects. Philosophy has to do with the direction of action. And these
two mental operations are radically different in kind.
The conclusions of the sciences are "grounded" in
evidence. The conclusions of philosophy are ungrounded, are "taken for granted." What then does it
mean to say that they are "based on knowledge"?

IV

In 1918, two years after the first edition of *Democracy
and Education*, Dewey gave a lecture at the University
of California, on the topic "Philosophy and Democracy." The problem of that lecture was the one which

[9] *Ibid.*, p. 376.
[10] *Loc. cit.*

we are now raising. What is the philosophic basis for that American choice of the democratic way of life which two years earlier Dewey had himself made? And the lecture is an explicit assertion of the arbitrariness, the ungroundedness, of the choice of democracy. The conclusions of philosophic criticism are, as such, made without reasonable justification.

As he seeks for evidence to support this sharp separation between the methods of science and those of philosophy Dewey finds the most striking feature of philosophies to be their multifariousness. While, in effect, there is only one science, there are many philosophies. They are ancient, medieval, and modern. They are English, French, or German. Some day, he tells us, when women have begun to do creative work in the field, we may even have a feminine philosophy as against the customary masculine ones.—We might add here the suggestion that women philosophers too may have their emotional differences, and so still further increase the number of philosophic systems.— And these differences of philosophy, Dewey tells us, express "not diversities of intellectual emphasis so much as incompatibilities of temperament and expectation."[11] They started "not from science, not from ascertained knowledge, but from moral convictions, and then resorted to the best knowledge and the best intellectual methods available in their day to give the form of demonstration to what was essentially an attitude of will, or a moral resolution to prize one mode of life more highly than another and the wish to persuade other men that this was the wise way of living."[12] Philosophy, Dewey says, comes into human living when men advance beyond the work of "knowing" into another kind of work. So long as we are engaged

[11] John Dewey, *Characters and Events* (New York: Holt, 1929), Vol. II, p. 843.
[12] *Ibid.*, p. 844.

in the sciences, we are truth-seeking. We are looking
for that which may be "recognized to be established
truth." But the theory of education is not striving for
truth. It is attempting to direct action. It arises, Dewey
tells us, when men meet the "need for projecting even
the completest knowledge upon a realm of another
dimension, namely, the dimension of action."[13] And
the driving, justifying force of that action is not
knowledge but will. "All philosophy bears an intellectual impress because it is an effort to convince some
one, perhaps the writer himself, of the reasonableness
of some course of life which has been adopted from
custom or instinct."[14] It may take the "garb" but not
the "form" of knowledge. And in this case, "scientific
form is a vehicle for conveying a non-scientific conviction, but the carriage is necessary, for philosophy is
not mere passion but a passion that would exhibit itself
as a reasonable persuasion."[15]

A "passion that would exhibit itself as a reasonable
persuasion"—that is Dewey's characterization of the
"general theory of education." That is the theoretical
basis which he has provided for American teaching.
Philosophies differ, we are told, because they arise in
different individuals and groups, from different moral
convictions, different attitudes of will. Those differences are not rational. Each philosophy has, as its
origin and final justification, a unique and distinct
moral conviction, a peculiar set of habits, customs, instincts. And from this it follows that philosophic principles are not intellectually justified or rejected. They
are subjectively preferred. They are cultural dogmas.
The advocates of these dogmas do not reason with one
another. The thinking of the philosopher is not reason-

13 *Ibid.*, p. 848.
14 *Ibid.*, p. 846.
15 *Ibid.*, p. 847.

ing. It is rhetoric. It is an attempt to give scientific form to that which is not scientific. It is to exhibit as a "reasonable persuasion" a "passion" which is not reasonable. It is an attempt to convince—not to know. It would "convince some one, perhaps the writer himself, of the reasonableness" of customs and habits and instincts which, in their very nature as such, have none of the quality of reasonableness. In a word, education has, as its theoretical basis, unreason, ungrounded and arbitrary choice.

V

Dewey's contention that "the general theory of education" is adopted without justification reaches its sharpest statement in the *Reconstruction in Philosophy*, published in 1920. In that controversial piece of arguing he opposes, "with malice prepense," science and philosophy, with constant disparagement of the latter. The attack upon philosophy, which runs through the book differs curiously in form, though not in intention from that of the paper on "Philosophy and Democracy." Philosophy is here regarded, not as the guide of action but rather as the maker of "general theories." The dominant motive of the book comes to focus in the last chapter, which deals with social philosophy. And the conclusion reached is explicit. It is unwise, Dewey tells us, to philosophize, to have and to use "general theories" of society. This statement presumably applies also to having "general theories" of education. "What is needed," Dewey says, "is specific inquiries into a multitude of specific structures and interactions. Not only does the solemn reiteration of categories of individual and organic or social whole not further these definite and detailed inquiries but it checks them. It detains thought within pompous and

sonorous generalities wherein controversy is as inevitable as it is incapable of solution."[16] Such theorizing
as this tends to substitute mere abstract ideas for concrete, specific investigations. Science, then, must take
charge of action. "We need guidance in dealing with
particular perplexities in domestic life and we are met
by dissertations on the Family or by assertions of the
Sacredness of Individual Personality."[17] The Dewey
who writes those words would seem to have little confidence in a "general theory of education." In his
hands, philosophy, as the search for wisdom, has fallen
upon evil days.

It is, however, obvious that what Dewey says in the
Reconstruction about the nature of philosophizing is
not, and could not be, his total judgment about the
business to which his own life has been devoted. What
he is condemning here is not "philosophy" but "bad
philosophy." After all, Dewey is not a scientist. He is
not an investigator. He is a philosopher, a generalizer,
a spinner of theories. As already noted, the range of his
abstractions takes in at one sweep the whole field of
human experience. And the attack of the *Reconstruction*, soberly considered, without "malice prepense,"
is directed, not at the use of generalizations, but at the
abuse of them. Dewey finds that social theorizing,
when not based in solid fact, has evil effects. It tends
to irrelevance and to dogmatism. It furnishes a way of
escape from actual problems. It also sanctifies the
status quo. And in these observations he is undoubtedly
right. These are the fruits of bad theorizing, pragmatic or non-pragmatic. Generalizations are dangerous
instruments. But what follows? Shall we cease from
using them? In the *Reconstruction* Dewey seems to be
very near to that generalization. Certainly his words

[16] John Dewey, *Reconstruction in Philosophy* (New York: Holt,
1920), pp. 198–199.
[17] *Ibid.*, p. 189.

suggest it. His discussion of social philosophy forbids any general theory of society. His whole argument is a defense of that negative attitude. And that means, for our argument, that he is also denying the possibility of a "general theory of education."

VI

The destructive effect of Dewey's subjective account of the process by which knowledge is used for the guidance of action has been, both for studies of society and for studies of education, enormous. Wherever that interpretation has been accepted, social attitudes, and educational policies, have been acknowledged to be founded in unreason. Reasoning, in all its practical phases, has been regarded as "rationalizing." When two "patterns of culture," such as democracy and aristocracy, face each other as rival claimants for the directing of a plan of education, as they do in the text of *Democracy and Education,* Dewey gives us no rational way of choosing between them by a fair, objective, impartial, disinterested measuring of their relative advantages. That choice is made, not by reasoning but by moral conviction, by custom, by habit, by instinct. When a society is divided into two social groups, the aristocrats and democrats, these parties are not, in any intellectual sense, in communication with one another. Each of them has "taken for granted" as its basic postulate a "general attitude" which, with equal lack of reason, is rejected by the opposing group. In that situation, there can be no objective attempt by co-operative intelligence to weigh the merits, under actual conditions, of the two basic assumptions. Neither group is criticizing its own postulates. Neither group is trying to understand the other. Each is busy in giving to its own dogma, and the practical consequences of that dogma, the form of demonstration which will make them plausible. This is the procedure which F. H. Bradley so cleverly characterizes when he defines metaphysics as "the finding of bad reasons for what we believe upon instinct," and adds, "but to find those reasons is no less an instinct."[18]

And, at this point, we must, in large measure, hold a subjective Dewey guilty of the charge of giving articulate expression, in the fields of social science and of education, to the belief that, in the last resort, all social thinking, as contrasted with the work of the "sciences," is irrational and dogmatic. It is a serious charge to make because I suppose no other doctrine has done so much to destroy the foundations of sober inquiry into social conditions and social programs as has the conviction that, in this field, men are not really inquiring but are only "assuming the garb" of doing so. They are not really co-operating in a common intellectual study. They are merely trying to "put something over" on another. As I read parts of *Democracy and Education* and all of "Philosophy and Democracy" and *Reconstruction in Philosophy*, Dewey is clearly on that ground. And the unfortunate feature of his American influence is that it is chiefly the Dewey of this mood who has been accepted as guide in the fields of education and of social science. From one end of America to the other we come upon men working in those two fields who use the notion of "rationalization" as a kind of patter, with apparently no realization of its implications as an account of what they themselves are doing. It is the members of this group who tell us that all teaching is, and must be, propaganda. In the process of developing the minds of their pupils, our teachers have available, they say, only the warring dogmas of conflicting sects, conflicting nations or cultures, each of which is fundamentally unintelligible to the others and

[18] F. H. Bradley, *Appearance and Reality* (London: Swan, Sonnenschein, 1893), Preface, xiv.

to itself. This being true, all that any teacher can do is to pick his own dogma, or obediently accept that of some social group to which he belongs, and proceed to find the most plausible ways of making that dogma acceptable to his pupils. And the irony of that situation is that the men who thus make "rationalizing" the fundamental term in teaching and in social theorizing almost invariably turn to Dewey as their master, regard him as the fountainhead of their wisdom.[19]

In so far as Dewey's writing has had that effect upon the social and educational activities of America it must be said that the pragmatic philosophy has failed to do what it undertook to do. Fifty years ago, the theologi-

[19] The extent to which this point of view has penetrated the field of social study and has destroyed the standards of moral judgment is suggested by the following words of Robert M. MacIver. Speaking of ethical principles he says, "But we discover soon enough that there is no body of accepted doctrine in respect of that problem, and that in the nature of the case there can be none. For if I say that happiness is the supreme end of life and another gainsays me, what way can be found of deciding between our claims? If I meant that men as a rule do seek happiness before everything else, my statement may admit of verification or refutation, but if I mean that what men *ought* to seek is happiness, how can that statement be controverted except by an equally dogmatic statement that they *ought not* to seek it? Now the distinctive character of ethics is that it is concerned with the question of *ought,* the question of right and wrong, good and bad. It is concerned, that is, with a question lying beyond the bounds of scientific procedure, beyond verification, beyond induction, beyond actuality. Therefore, we can have a history of ethics but no science of it. Instead of a science we must be content with a philosophy—or rather a series of philosophies, varying according to the insight and character of each philosopher, a series whose ethical contradictions and antagonisms can never be dissolved by any scientific procedure. All ethical claims are claims of worthfulness, and we can neither confirm nor refute them save by our own estimate of their worth. In so far as they may mistake the true relation of means to ends, in so far as they may maintain that a system or mode of action contributes to some end to which in fact it does not contribute, we may convict them of scientific error, but in so far as they maintain that an end is good *in itself,* how shall we refute them if we disbelieve—save by denial?" R. M. MacIver, *Community* (New York: Macmillan, 1920), pp. 55–56.

cal answer to the question, "What is objective, critical
intelligence?" had lost its meaning. The new naturalism
offered to provide, out of the findings of biology, a
new answer to replace the old one. But the answer
which the *Reconstruction in Philosophy* gives is
"There is no objective, critical intelligence." Intelligence is, as such, subjective and uncritical. The outcome of Dewey's search for "a general theory of
education" is that general theories are not worth having.
As we shall see later, this conclusion is hostile to many
of Dewey's deepest convictions. And yet he never
abandons it. And what is worse, it is this side of his
thinking which has been popularly known and widely
accepted. So far as his general influence is concerned,
the outcome of his attempt to make human behavior
critically and objectively intelligent is the belief that
the activity which we call intelligence is neither critical nor objective nor intelligent. A philosophy of life
is "a passion that would exhibit itself as a reasonable
persuasion."—It is a strange conclusion to be reached
by a man whose dominant motive has been to raise the
studies of human behavior to a level co-ordinate with
that of the physical sciences.

VII

We have thus far followed Dewey's discussion of the
relation between knowledge and intelligence in what
may be called his subjective mood. But as already
noted, Dewey has also another mood, an objective one.
His values are not only "valued." They are also "evaluated," that is, critically estimated.[20] The ideas of philosophy, though based on passion, are yet also based on
knowledge. And for this second mood, such choices as
that of democracy are not merely arbitrary. They are

[20] John Dewey, *Logic, The Theory of Inquiry* (New York: Holt,
1938), p. 173.

subjected to critical examination. They are established, modified, repudiated, as they meet, or fail to meet, the tests of criticism. Dewey intends to have an objective criterion by the use of which such choices can be tested.

From the pages of *The Quest for Certainty, Experience and Nature, Art as Experience, Logic, the Theory of Inquiry,* we could select dozens of passages in which this work of critical intelligence is assigned to the philosophic mind. Dewey still separates the fields of knowledge and of action. But philosophy is no longer confined to the latter and excluded from the former. It now deals with the relations between the two. And, that being true, it acquires a status which is independent both of knowledge and of action. It becomes a third party, a referee or judge, who can criticize and evaluate both what men know and what they do. It has authority to bring the knowledge of science and the values of action into right relations to one another.

In the *Quest for Certainty,* for example, Dewey says, "Man has beliefs which scientific inquiry vouchsafes, beliefs about the actual structure and processes of things; and he has also beliefs[21] about the values which should regulate his conduct. The question of how these two ways of believing may most effectively and fruitfully interact with one another is the most general and significant problem which life presents to us. Some reasoned discipline, one obviously other than any science, should deal with this issue."[22]—It is a far cry from the "passion that would exhibit itself as a reasonable persuasion," to that statement which makes the pursuit of philosophic intelligence, a "reasoned disci-

[21] Note that Dewey here speaks not of "values" but of "beliefs about values." The immediate product of philosophy is not "action" but a "theory of action."

[22] John Dewey, *The Quest for Certainty* (New York: Minton, Balch, 1929), pp. 18–19.

pline" which is "other than any science" and which
yet deals with "the most general and significant problem which life presents to us." This does not sound
like "taking things for granted."

And again we read,[23] "The problem of restoring integration and co-operation between man's beliefs about
the world in which he lives and his beliefs about the
values and purposes that should direct his conduct is
the deepest problem of modern life." And still again,
in *Experience and Nature*,[24] Dewey gives to philosophic thinking a description which marks it off both
from active behavior and from the inquiries of the
special sciences. "These remarks are preparatory to
presenting a conception of philosophy: namely, that
philosophy is inherently criticism, having its distinctive position among various modes of criticism in its
generality: a criticism of criticisms, as it were." And
later we read, "And this effort to make our desires, our
striving and our ideals (which are as natural to man as
his aches and his clothes) articulate, to define them
(not in themselves which is impossible) in terms of inquiry into conditions and consequences is what I have
called criticism and, when carried on in the grand
manner, philosophy."[25]

VIII

In later chapters we must examine how Dewey uses
this second method of criticism. That method, too,
we must see in action. For the moment, however, our
concern is with the fact that there are two methods,
that Dewey has given us two different accounts of the
search for intelligence. And, as they are stated, those

---

[23] *Ibid.,* p. 255.
[24] *Loc cit.* (Chicago: Open Court, 1925), p. 398.
[25] *Ibid.,* 418.

accounts are radically opposed to one another. For the first, intelligence is "based in passion." For the second, it is the product of criticism. In the paper on "Philosophy and Democracy," the task of philosophy is to "exhibit as reasonable" convictions which are adopted from "custom and instinct." Such beliefs start "not from science, not from ascertained knowledge, but from moral convictions." But in the *Quest for Certainty* and *Experience and Nature*, philosophy has become "a reasoned discipline" whose business is "criticism." In the first case, the attempt of intelligence is to "convince," to "persuade." In the other, it is an activity of "inquiry." In the argument of *Democracy and Education*, a social program is "taken for granted." When Dewey is in his objective mood, all social programs are to be "justified" and "criticized" by an "inquiry into conditions and consequences." Philosophy which, at first, had only the "garb" of reason has now taken on its "form." The phrase "exact of us" has acquired meaning.

I am not saying that these two points of view are wholly irreconcilable. It is obvious that when Dewey makes these different statements, he is, in different moods, looking at different aspects of the human situation. But the difficulty is that those differences are not clearly recognized. And the resulting total impression is one of confusion and incoherence.

IX

The depth of the ambiguity of which we are speaking was revealed in a recent interchange of criticism and reply between Dewey and Joseph Ratner. The latter tells us that he has found "a fundamental fault (geologically speaking) which lies deep in the instrumentalism in *Studies in Logical Theory* (1903)." Quoting

from *The Need for a Recovery of Philosophy* (1925)
Dewey's statement that "the pragmatic notion of reality is precisely that no theory of Reality in general,
überhaupt, is possible or needed," Ratner says, "Here
more explicitly than in our earlier examples we find
Dewey going from the proposition that there is no
'Reality in general' (which is true) to the conclusion
that no general theory of reality is possible (which is
false). The passage cited," he continues, "may right-
fully be claimed as itself a nuclear or germinal statement of a general theory of reality. But it is quite
unnecessary to argue the point. Just as Dewey in *The
Public and Its Problems* thoroughly corrected the idea
that a general theory of the state and society is not
necessary by developing one, so in *Experience and
Nature*, which appeared some eight years after the
citation above was written, he explicitly developed a
general 'theory of nature, of the world, of the universe.' "[26]

Now Ratner's criticism at this point seems to me
warranted. Dewey does contradict himself on the question of general theories. He both denies their validity
and uses them as valid. And yet Ratner's dealing with
the "fault" is not fully satisfactory. He tells us that
Dewey has "thoroughly corrected" an error by urging
its opposite. The assertion that we cannot have general
theories is disposed of by the producing of two such
general theories. But surely that "correction" is not
very "thorough." Dewey, we are told, has continued
to make two contradictory assertions. In adopting the
second, which Ratner approves, he has not abandoned
the first, which Ratner condemns, even though the
second is a denial of the first. If the second is true, then
the line of reasoning by which the first was established

[26] *The Philosophy of John Dewey,* The Library of Living Philosophers, Vol. I, 1939, p. 66.

must have been faulty at some essential point. And correction would be the discovery and elimination of that fault. But that, so far as Ratner tells us, so far as any reader of Dewey can tell us, has not been done. The two contradictory assertions are left face to face, irreconcilable and yet both accepted. And as a result the whole discussion of "general ideas" remains involved in confusion and uncertainty. Dewey both condemns their use and uses them.

But Dewey's reply to Ratner gives even more striking evidence of the ambiguity in which his study of knowledge and intelligence is involved. In self-defense, Dewey says, "I did not hit upon my position as a ready made and finished doctrine. It developed in and through a series of reactions to a number of philosophic problems. Under these conditions," he continues, "it is natural that inconsistencies and shifts have taken place: the most I can claim is that I have moved fairly steadily in one direction." And then, in characterizing that direction, Dewey makes one of the most startling suggestions ever made by a writer on philosophy. He suggests that in the course of his lifelong discussion "knowledge" and "intelligence" may have been confused, may, at times, have changed places. "Dr. Ratner," he says, "is quite right in indicating that the word *intelligence* represents what is essential in my view much better than does the word *knowledge,* while it avoids the confusion of knowing—inquiry— and attained knowledge which has led some of my critics astray in their accounts of my position. At present, after reading criticisms of the kind of *instrumentalism* that is attributed to me, it is clear that I should, from the start, have systematically distinguished between knowledge as the outcome of special inquiries (undertaken because of the presence of problems) and *intelligence* as the product and expression of cumulative funding of the meanings[27] reached in these special cases."[28]

The effect of that "explanation" upon one who has for many years been trying to understand Dewey's "general theory of education," who has seen that the whole structure of his thought has to do with the relation between "knowledge" and "intelligence," is simply devasting. It is as if Kant should have said, looking back upon his *Critiques*, "Dr. X. is quite right in saying that *a priori* represents what is essential in my view much better than does *a posteriori*. I should from the start have distinguished between them. It was, of course, the latter which I meant when I spoke of the former." For the fact is that Dewey has always distinguished between knowledge and intelligence. From the beginning, his structure of ideas rests on that distinction. It is the crux of all he has to say about the philosophy of society and, hence, of the theory of education. If, as he now tells us, there has been confusion at this point, if one of these terms may be substituted for the other, that confusion goes so deep that no mere abstract redefining or interchanging of the two terms will correct it. There must be radical rethinking of

[27] The phrase "the cumulative funding of meanings" covers a nest of technical difficulties with which this argument cannot deal. It suggests that, in some way or other, after a scientific inquiry is finished, it leaves behind it "meanings" which are "funded." Apparently those meanings are stored away, are kept available for further use by the sciences or philosophy. It would be hard to imagine a more tantalizingly elusive notion than this. Do meanings exist when not in active use? If that is true, its implications for education are very important and strongly counter to the general drift of Dewey's influence.—But the issue is too technical for discussion here. To any reader who wishes to pursue it I would recommend as a starting point, the brilliant study of Dewey's "Epistemology and Metaphysics" by A. E. Murphy in the *Philosophy of John Dewey,* and Dewey's reply to the question there raised. Murphy doubts whether "inquiry" as Dewey describes it, leaves behind it any cognitive meanings, which might be funded or used.

[28] Dewey, "Experience, Knowledge and Value: a Rejoinder," in Schillp, *op. cit.,* pp. 520–521.

the total set of ideas in which those terms are involved. That rethinking has not been done. And the resulting confusion in this interpretation of the work of our schools and colleges has been disastrous. Every teacher knows, as Dewey assures us, that knowledge must be used for the creating of intelligence. No one denies that. But the question for which we need an answer is "By what process of thinking is knowledge transformed into wisdom?" What is that activity of philosophy or criticism or intelligence which the teacher must attempt to set up in the mind of his pupil? Dewey gives us two conflicting views of that activity. And the difference between those views is decisive for any theory of education. Is intelligence a procedure for rationalizing our passions? Or is it a procedure by which practical beliefs are tested by objective intellectual criticism? Dewey says both of these. And the result of that ambiguity is that, in the social sciences, in the schools and colleges, which have been influenced by Dewey's leadership, the notion of intelligence is a vague and ineffectual one. No one, in his generation, has pressed more strongly than Dewey the claims of critical thinking. But it is equally true that no one has done more to involve those claims in uncertainty and confusion.

RELEVANT READING

The many references cited by Professor Meiklejohn should serve the reader who wishes to pursue his arguments.

Educational Liberalism
and Dewey's Philosophy

❀

Israel Scheffler

Though criticism of American education is decidedly
no new historical phenomenon, few reflective persons
underestimate the severity of the current phase. Nor,
while acknowledging its complex roots, do they fail
to see its connection with the general regression from
liberalism currently in evidence. Within this development, it is not surprising that the educational doctrines
of John Dewey, our outstanding recent spokesman of
liberalism, should again have become centers of dispute. It is, however, unfortunate that for many concerned with education his work has become an
unanalyzable symbol, to be attacked as a whole or
defended as a whole, rather than to be studied carefully and independently evaluated. In particular, if
we accept Sidney Hook's characterization of Dewey's
educational liberalism as involving essentially (a) the
application of scientific research and criticism to educational practice, and (b) the application of democratic values and principles to the reform of such
practice and its associated institutions and habits of
mind, then it seems to me especially unfortunate for
proponents of such liberalism to feel that it must
always be defended in the context of Dewey's general

This selection originally appeared in the *Harvard Educational Review,* Spring, 1956. Mr. Scheffler is Professor of Philosophy and
Education at Harvard University.

philosophy. For, aside from considerations of strategy hinging on the fact that such liberalism may validly be supported on widely differing philosophic grounds, I think that certain features of Dewey's general position are independently weak and contribute irrelevant difficulties to the defense of educational liberalism.

In the discussion to follow, then, I shall try to explain and support this judgment by (1) briefly sketching Dewey's view of intelligence and learning, (2) discussing some of his dominant emphases in education, and (3) setting forth certain strictures on the foregoing, and related parts of Dewey's philosophy. For the brevity of my treatment of (1) and (2), I offer only as a minor reason the limitations of space. More important is the fact that I am here less interested in the meticulous interpretation of Dewey's intentions and the development of his thought than in the objective significance of certain of his recurrent models, metaphors, and key concepts as these have influenced educators. And, since a definitive reading of such a complex writer will in any event be lacking for a long time, I can only urge those who question mine to join me in considering the merits of the influential doctrines to be discussed, whatever their eventual fate at the hands of historians and biographers.

DEWEY'S VIEW OF INTELLIGENCE AND LEARNING

Dewey's basic modes of thought and argumentation are holistic. A favorite tactic is to interpret the given problem as generated by some philosophic dualism and then to deal with the latter not by adopting one or another of its sides exclusively but rather by showing the partiality of each and the continuity relating both within some inclusive framework. Though such philosophizing is, of course, not new, Dewey's use is

distinctive in its close dependence on modern science
both for specific findings and as the key model of an
evolving framework within which partial and conflicting views grow into unified and organic wholes.
His key philosophic terms "interaction," "transaction,"
"situation," reveal his organic tendency and his organic
view of science is given in his definition, "Inquiry is
the controlled or directed transformation of an in-
determinate situation into one that is so determinate
in its constituent distinctions and relations as to convert the elements of the original situation into a unified whole."[1]

Indeed, Dewey's basic philosophic purpose, as revealed in his various writings, may be said to have
been the overcoming of inherited and pervasive dualisms between science and morals, theory and practice,
mind and body, thought and action, means and ends.
To this purpose he develops a special concept of *experience*, reflecting distinctive features of the deliberate *experimentation* of the scientist, and quite different
from ordinary ideas of experience as just what goes on,
or what is passively beheld by someone. Experience,
for Dewey, is rather the result of an *interaction* between objective conditions and organic energies, and
is educative, as scientific experimentation is ideally, to
the extent that it engages the active deliberation,
imagination, and motivation of the organism.

To determine the educative potential of experience
in any context, Dewey generalizes the features of experimental research as the best-accredited source of
current knowledge. Such research is not random or
routine, but originates in a difficulty, a conflict, an unsettled situation constituting a problem. Hypotheses
are generated relative to this problem. Such hypotheses

[1] John Dewey, *Logic: The Theory of Inquiry* (New York: Holt,
1938), p. 104.

are not final ends but serve as guides for subsequent activity such as observation, data-processing, manipulation, inference; furthermore these hypotheses are controlled by the outcomes of such activity, i.e., they may turn out warranted and the original problem resolved, or they may prove unwarranted and the original difficulty remain to generate further hypotheses. The settlement of a problematic situation proceeds thus in two phases: *trying* in which we engage in deliberate activity guided by ideas, and *undergoing* in which we attend to the consequences of this activity as a control over such ideas. Where these ideas survive the test reliably, they may be taken as embodying an accurate perception of relations between our activity and associated consequences, a perception rendered general and usable in a wide variety of future circumstances by its ideal formulation. It is the growth of such perceptions which renders the environment increasingly meaningful and which, applied toward the control of activity, informs it increasingly with intelligence, and weights it with responsibility. With the increasing responsibility accompanying intelligent control, subjection to blind habit and yielding to whim become avoidable and, indeed, morally wrong for greater and greater areas of our behavior. For the function of intelligence is to *reconstruct* practice by deliberately and imaginatively resolving problems as they occur, i.e. in a way that is more efficient than either stereotyped repetition or random variation in response.

When Dewey's philosophy of experience is put in more directly educational terms, it asserts that all genuine reflection, from the most rudimentary to the most highly abstract, exemplifies a single pattern. It always has its origin in a problem, a blocking of habitual conduct. The energy of outwardly unreleased habits is "turned inwards" to produce deliberation, a

dramatic rehearsal of possible future actions to meet
the problem. This "inner" drama continues until some
rehearsed consequence of some possible course sparks
"outward" activity once more, an activity whose reconstruction of conditions may succeed in overcoming
the initial block so as to allow once more a smooth
flow of behavior. The mind is not passive but active
and impulsive throughout the process. Its selectivity
helps determine the precise character of the problem,
its energy vitalizes the play of ideas, stimulates the re-
birth of activity and the consequent reconstruction
of conditions. Indeed, there is no longer any sense
in speaking of the mind as a separate entity, since no
line can be drawn between its functions and the rest of
the organism, nor indeed, between it and the environment. Its selectivity is one with the specific nature of
the organism, its energy is continuous with the mo-
mentum of past habit and with the rechanneled force
of new traits and conditions. It is best seen as a certain
functioning of the organism, a mode of conduct. There
is, then, no split between intelligence and conduct; intelligence is the control of conduct by meaning, i.e.
by its perceived consequences, while all conduct is
potentially intelligent. The only significant difference
that remains is that which separates routine or capri-
cious conduct from conduct intelligently governed by
a perception of its meaning. The notion of *technique*
is, moreover, not to be identified with blind routine
behavior and opposed to intelligence. Technique controlled by meaning is just meaning rendered effective;
it is the very opposite of mere routine and is exemplified ideally in the artist. "The artist is a masterful
technician. The technique or mechanism is fused with
thought and feeling. The mechanical performer permits the mechanism to dictate the performance. It is
absurd to say that the latter exhibits habit and the

former not. We are confronted with two kinds of habit, intelligent and routine."[2]

DEWEY'S DOMINANT EMPHASES IN EDUCATION

Dewey's holism and his emphasis on continuity find explicit application in his treatment of formal education. He opposes strongly any radical division between major branches or types of learning. The usual separation between higher and lower studies, between theoretical and applied sciences, between humanistic and vocational programs he considers an embodiment of the discredited divorce of intelligence from conduct. As rationality is not the exercise of a separate faculty, so enlightenment is not the exclusive result of contact with "pure" studies capable of engaging such a faculty. Education must, to render intelligence most effective, bring the studies together rather than perpetuating their separateness. It should exhibit technical and vocational studies in their theoretical setting, and should draw attention to their human and social import. Likewise, theoretical and literary studies should be related to the problems of men which they may illuminate, and the technical conditions of their growth or application.

Furthermore, the very division between the school and life outside the school, between learning and living, is one which needs to be overcome. It is based on the idea that the school can, in isolation, provide pure knowledge during a specified interval so as to prepare the student for a lifetime of informed action. But this idea ignores the fact that learning *is* living, that it takes place most effectively, moreover, in live

[2] John Dewey, *Human Nature and Conduct* (New York: Modern Library, 1930), p. 71, italics mine.

contexts which set real problems and call forth real
purposes, that the one significant way to integrate the
work of the school is not through mechanical devices
but by relating all of it to the life of the wider community.

Finally, Dewey's view stresses not only the continuity among the studies and between the school and
life, but also and most fundamentally, the continuity
between the specific truth deliberately taught and the
wider context of purpose, activity, and social environment in which its meaning becomes manifest to the
learner. The teacher must always remember that learning is not passive reception but involves, at its best,
active participation governed by perception of meanings in a problematic situation. This means that the
whole environment of meanings surrounding the lesson
is important as potentially contributing to learning. It
means, for example, that the moral atmosphere of the
classroom, the encouragement of curiosity and ques-
tioning, the relations among students and with the
teacher are to be considered, not as irrelevant to the
curriculum, but as the very basis of the moral and intellectual learning which goes on in the school
whether we deliberately plan it or not. It means,
finally, that every item of subject-matter to be taught
must be provided with context in the learner's perceptions. These perceptions and, indeed, the learner's
whole system of motivations must be taken with the
utmost seriousness by the teacher. Problems set within
this context activate real purposes and interest, challenge genuine effort and discipline important capacities.
"Study is effectual in the degree in which the pupil
realizes the place of the truth he is dealing with in
carrying to fruition activities in which he is concerned.
This connection of an object and a topic with the
promotion of an activity having a purpose is the first

and the last word of a genuine theory of interest in education."[3]

TWO CRITICISMS OF DEWEY'S APPROACH

The power, simplicity, and sensitivity of Dewey's thought on social and educational issues is undeniable. The force of his observations on teaching and learning is immediate, and even where he may be thought wrong in detail, few will deny the suggestiveness of his treatments. As to educational liberalism, there is no doubt that his case for the moral and educational relevance of science and the primacy of critical and democratic values in education is impressive. His way of looking at things together which are commonly held apart, of seeing continuities where others take gaps for granted, must be held a fruitful philosophical approach, justified by its consequences in his own work.

Yet it does have its dangers, and these must be noted despite the persuasive attractiveness of his closely knit system of ideas. To begin with, his very seeing of all things together and, moreover, always in relation to the future condition of man is likely to be too constricting a philosophic stance for many. Dewey's approach, I think, often runs the risk of mistaking valid distinctions for "divorces," "splits," and "sharp divisions" to be uniformly washed away, and his overwhelming social and moral concern leads him to underestimate the value of detachment from environing social conditions. Regarding the latter, Bertrand Russell, for example, remarks, "Dr. Dewey's world, it seems to me, is one in which human beings occupy the imagination; the cosmos of astronomy, though of course acknowledged to exist, is at most times

[3] John Dewey, *Democracy and Education* (New York: Macmillan, 1919), p. 158.

ignored."[4] Both dangers of his approach may be illustrated in connection with two distinctions which Dewey strongly criticizes. These distinctions, it seems to me, are not only aids to clarity, but worth preserving for the educational values to which they draw attention.

1. Consider Dewey's extended arguments against the "divorce" of ideas from action, of theory from practice. Presumably the point relates to the analysis of experiment, discussed above, according to which theoretical ideas arise out of disorganized practical situations and guide further activities by whose outcomes they are controlled. Thus the very function of ideas is to transform action and, consequently, the environment. "Ideas are worthless except as they pass into actions which rearrange and reconstruct in some way, be it little or large, the world in which we live."[5] Dewey's polemic against divorcing theory from practice may be construed as an attack upon ideas which are worthless in the sense indicated.

Now Dewey's view seems in great part motivated by emphasis on the empirical control over ideas in science, and what he opposes is the irresponsible assertion of claims unwarranted by empirical evidence. But his conception of the nature of empirical control is, it seems to me, unduly narrow, and fails to do justice to abstract, theoretical considerations in the scientific assessment of evidence. Ideas in science are not all of one kind and only certain simple types can be analyzed as instruments for transforming the world. With the growth of complicated theoretical structures, funda-

[4] Bertrand Russell, *A History of Western Philosophy* (New York: Simon & Schuster, 1945), p. 827.

[5] John Dewey, *The Quest for Certainty* (New York: Minton, 1929), p. 138. Dewey's complete sentence is, "For then mankind will learn that, intellectually (that is, save for the esthetic enjoyment they afford, which is of course a true value), ideas are worthless except as . . ."

mental statements in science can no longer be understood in the same way. They do not refer to our
common world, which is describable by empirical
evidence, and they do not, in themselves, guide our
activities at all. It is only the whole many-leveled
structures in which they are embedded which tie up,
at sporadic points, with our world of evidence and
action. Since they must moreover, meet such requirements as simplicity, formulation in acceptable terms,
naturalness, likelihood of connection with other structures etc., their superiority over alternatives within
given systems is often not a question of systematic
superiority in "passing into actions which reconstruct
the world in which we live," but is judged in purely
theoretical terms.

Dewey's emphasis on empirical control is perhaps
then best expressed if we take his above statement to
refer, not to single theories, but to whole systematic
structures themselves. Granting that parts of such
structures need not themselves connect up with our
world, we may interpret him as insisting that the whole
structures must make connection, though purely theoretical considerations indeed enter into their design
and acceptance.

Nevertheless, there remains an ambiguity in the notion of "our world" or, as Dewey puts it, "the world
in which we live." For though this phrase is indeed
often used to refer to the world in which we here,
now, and in the foreseeable future live and act, our
scientific systems connect up with various segments
of a world which is indefinitely wider in scope, a
world to which the same phrase may also be construed
to refer. To argue, from the way in which scientific
systems significantly connect up with this wide world,
against ideas which fail to tie up with our limited
future world of practice would be clearly fallacious.

If we now leave the realm of scientific logic and ask

what *educational* value could possibly reside in such ideas, it seems to me that it is just their transcendence of our own practical environment which enables them to enlarge the intellectual perspectives of the student. What is of questionable educational value is trivial, petty, narrow learning, not theoretical study which, though illuminating broad reaches of our world, is without practical reference for our own present and future problems. If such study is thus, at least partly, the task of the school, then the school *ought* to stand apart from life in a basic sense: not by cultivating pedantry or myth, but by illuminating a wider world than its limited surroundings and by sustaining those habits of mind which fit it for breadth, penetration, and objectivity of vision. It is not, of course, implied that the school ought not therefore to provide specific preparation for life in the practical future of its pupils. But even where subject-matter is taught primarily for its future practical value, students will miss something of high importance if they learn it solely *for the sake of* this practical value. It is important even here for the school to maintain its *autonomous* standards of evaluation by cultivating, as far as possible, an independent appreciation of subject-matter and a capacity for purely theoretical curiosity and dispassionate vision.

2. Consider now Dewey's unified approach to reflective thinking and knowledge, his denial in effect that we can validly distinguish between the descriptive and the instrumental functions of thought. In line with this approach, he attacks conceptions of science as providing fixed ideas which reflect "antecedent existences," knowledge which "is a disclosure of reality . . . prior to and independent of knowing."[6] He insists rather on the problem origin of all thinking, on the consequences of reflection within specific situations, on the

[6] *Ibid.,* p. 44.

functioning of knowledge in life. "The two limits of every unit of thinking are a perplexed, troubled, or confused situation at the beginning and a cleared-up, unified, resolved situation at the close. The first of these situations may be called *pre*-reflective. It sets the problem to be solved; out of it grows the question that reflection has to answer. In the final situation the doubt has been dispelled; the situation is *post*-reflective; there results a direct experience of mastery, satisfaction, enjoyment. Here, then, are the limits within which reflection falls."[7]

From such a conception of thinking stems the educational emphasis on the purposes, needs, and sensitivities of the child as forming the basic context of learning, since setting the problems which may best motivate reflection. From this conception taken together with the opposition to "fixity" of ideas comes the natural educational proposal to reorganize traditional blocks of subject-matter around problems arising out of felt needs and purposes in life contexts. Now it is nonsense (and Dewey recognized it as such) to appeal to children's transient needs and purposes as a criterion of our long-range educational goals and their associated choices of subject-content. Hence the emphasis on such needs and purposes is, I think, best taken as *methodological* advice, logically independent from long-range choice of content-goals, and warranted by the assumption that learning is more efficient as it is directed within *problematic situations from the child's standpoint.*

Now, as thus methodologically conceived, such advice has undeniable relevance for much of our formal education. Yet, taken by itself, it seems to me much too narrow, in effect opposing the "fixity" of ideas only to replace it by a "fixity" of problems. Even insofar as it bases itself on the model of scientific inquiry,

[7] John Dewey, *How We Think* (Boston: Heath, 1910), p. 106.

the attack on fixity of ideas, on knowledge as disclosure of independent existence, seems to me obviously absurd in confusing *facts* with *our attempts to
ascertain them, truth* with *confirmation at a given
time*.[8] Unless science purports to estimate the facts
about events and processes prior to, later than, and
independent of our knowing, in quite clear and basic
senses, it is a puny enterprise indeed; this is independent of the fact that its *estimates* themselves are obviously neither prior to, later than, nor independent of
its estimation, nor fixed in the sense of being immune
to revision over time.

But what reason do we have for assimilating all reflective thinking to the problem-solving model in
general? In ordinary speech, for example, the poet is
thinking in the process of composition, the artist in
creation, the translator in attempting a translation, and
yet none is seeking the answer to a question.[9] Though
subsidiary questions need to be answered in the course
of each activity, no *answer* or *set of answers* as such
brings each activity to a unified and resolved close;
only a satisfactory poem, painting, or translation will
do. And what is happening when I on certain occasions
think long enough to discover that I have been working on a pseudo-problem? If I am right, then though
I was genuinely thinking, my thought grew out of
no problem at all. Of course, it will be said that though
it grew out of no intelligible *question* it was prompted
by uneasiness. But such argument reduces the problem-solving approach to triviality. For aside from the
difficulty of distinguishing between *intellectual* uneasiness and the discomfort of e.g. a cold,—strongly

[8] Or, as we may also say, *truth* with *certainty*. See, for example,
Dewey's statement in *Human Nature and Conduct,* p. 236, "Behind
however the conception of fixity whether in science or morals lay
adherence to certainty of 'truth,' a clinging to something fixed, etc."
[9] For a discussion of this point, see G. Ryle's treatment of thinking in *Acta Psychologica,* 1953.

motivated daydreams and metaphysical constructions will turn out instances of inquiry in the problem-solving, allegedly scientific sense.

The emphasis on the initial problematic contexts of the learner, even from a methodological point-of-view, seems to me to underplay certain important *educational* values, moreover. Foremost among these is the creation of new problems for the learner, the introduction of *unsettled* situations where none existed before. No matter how broadly we may conceive the problems supposed to initiate reflective thinking, that is, our educational purpose is to *create wider perception* as well as to *improve thinking* taken as the settlement of problems. We do not approach our educational tasks within the limits of problems alone, but also with standards of relative importance of problems and we use these as guides to creating perceptions which are broader than those of the learner; it is here that perhaps the traditional subjects and standards serve most clearly.

Nor is this an unimportant point generally, for liberalism. For as our culture increasingly distracts us, it becomes easier and easier to avoid significant problems rather than face them head-on, increasingly possible to stifle our momentary perceptions of evils, especially when remote, and concentrate instead on narrow and personal problems. It is, then, well to remember, especially in our theorizing about education for freedom, that such freedom involves broad and alert perception as well as efficient problem-solving, ability to search out disjointed and unfitting elements in experience, as well as the drive to unify, organize, and settle.

Obviously, of course, I do not for one moment impute to Dewey himself either failure in perception or lack of general recognition of its significance in education. No one who has read him can do this. But I *am* suggesting that some of his basic models in philosophy, and his specific conceptions of inquiry and learning are wrong in certain respects, and that the defense of educational liberalism should not be burdened with their defects. Insofar as the cultivation of free habits of mind is educationally of the first importance, there is little argument. If I have, nonetheless, misread Dewey in the opinions of some, I hope that the issues raised will be considered on their own merits and will, furthermore, stimulate the kind of detailed and analytic discussion of his work which alone signifies that it is being taken seriously, in place of the ritualistic use of his name in educational dispute.

RELEVANT READING

Dewey, John, *The Way Out of Educational Confusion*. Cambridge, Massachusetts: Harvard University Press, 1931.
—— "Science as Subject Matter and as Method." *Science*, N. S. XXXI (January 28, 1910).
—— *The Influence of Darwin on Philosophy and Other Essays in Contemporary Thought*. New York: Henry Holt & Company, Inc., 1910.
—— *Democracy and Education*. New York: The Macmillan Company, 1916.
—— *How We Think*. Boston: D. C. Heath & Company, 1910.
—— *Experience and Education*. New York: The Macmillan Company, 1938.
Lynch, Jarmon A., "Concerning the Emphasis on Methods." *Journal of Philosophy*, XXXVII (May 9, 1940).
Peirce, Charles S., "The Fixation of Belief." *Popular Science Monthly*, XII (November, 1877).
Scheffler, Israel, *The Language of Education*. Springfield: Charles C. Thomas, Publisher, 1960.
—— *Philosophy and Education*. Boston: Allyn & Bacon, 1958.
—— "Justifying Curriculum Decisions." *The School Review*. Chicago: The University of Chicago Press, 1958.

The Educational Theory of John Dewey

Charles D. Hardie

There is little doubt that the writings of Dewey have had more influence on educational theory than those of any other living thinker. Nevertheless, they are often obscure and are sometimes inconsistent with each other. It is, therefore, difficult to give a clear and coherent exposition of what his educational theory is, and while it is easy to criticize many of his actual statements it is often difficult to be sure that it is not just the statement but also the theory which is at fault.

The philosophic basis of Dewey's theory is what has been called "Pragmatism" by philosophers. This doctrine, which has been advocated by such eminent men as William James and F. C. S. Schiller, has had much greater popularity in America than in Europe. It is a doctrine concerning the nature of our knowledge. "If ideas, meanings, conceptions, notions, theories, systems are instrumental to an active reorganization of the given environment, to a removal of some specific trouble and perplexity, then the test of their validity and value lies in accomplishing this work. If they succeed in their office, they are reliable, sound, valid, good, true. If they fail to clear up confusion, to eliminate defects, if they increase confusion, uncertainty and evil when they are acted upon, then they are

This selection originally appeared as a chapter in *Truth and Fallacy in Educational Theory,* 1942. Mr. Hardie is a Professor of Education at the University of Tasmania.

false. . . . The hypothesis that works is the *true* one; and *truth* is an abstract noun applied to the collection of cases, actual, foreseen and devised, that receive confirmation in their works and consequences."[1]

Pragmatism was conclusively refuted by Professor G. E. Moore as far back as 1908,[2] and I shall discuss it very briefly lest the philosophic reader should consider me sadistic in flogging what is undoubtedly a dead horse. On the other hand, many writers on education seem to be quite unaware of the arguments against it.

Moore distinguishes four propositions, all of which Pragmatists wish to assert, and which are implicit in the above quotation from Dewey. These propositions are:

(1) We can verify all those of our ideas which are true.

(2) All those among our ideas, which we can verify, are true.

(3) All our true ideas are useful.

(4) All those of our ideas which are useful are true.

The only proposition of these four which Moore accepts is (2), and for the arguments against the other three, the reader should refer to Moore's paper. Moore's arguments appear to me to be quite irrefutable, and it may well be asked, does not Pragmatism state something else apart from these four propositions? It is difficult to say, as those writers who profess Pragmatism rarely state the theory any more clearly than Dewey does in the above quotation. Nevertheless, I believe that most Pragmatists subscribe to the view

[1] John Dewey, *Reconstruction in Philosophy* (New York: Holt, 1920), pp. 156–157.

[2] G. E. Moore, "Professor James's Pragmatism," *Proceedings of the Aristotelian Society* (1907–1908).

which William James expressed in the words "our truths are man-made products,"[3] and there does seem to me to be a sense in which this is both true and important.

Hobbes once wrote, "True and False are attributes of Speech not of things, and where Speech is not, there is neither Truth nor Falsehood." This asserts, what is certainly the case, that truth is bound up with language. If language did not exist, then the characteristic denoted by "true" (not merely the word "true") would not exist; and since language is a man-made product, it follows that in some sense truth is a man-made product. Let us try, therefore, to become clearer as to how truth is bound up with language. Language is used by man for a number of purposes of which the following are perhaps the most important:[4]

(1) To communicate information.

(2) To arouse feelings (as in propaganda and some types of poetry).

(3) To direct people and animals (as in commands).

(4) To express feelings (as in some types of poetry and exclamations).

Now the only use of language with which truth is connected is the first, and the essential unit involved in that use is the proposition. This is what has led many philosophers to assert that it is only propositions which can be true or false. Other units of language such as questions, commands, etc., are not related to truth or falsity. Language in this first use consists of a set of symbols (vocabulary), and a set of rules. The

[3] Moore discusses this point in the paper mentioned, but the discussion does not seem to me to be as good as the rest of the paper.

[4] Compare C. K. Ogden and I. A. Richards, *The Meaning of Meaning* (London: International Library of Psychology, Philosophy, and Scientific Method, 1923), pp. 224–227.

rules are of two kinds:[5] (*a*) formation rules, or rules
which explain how propositions are to be formed from
the vocabulary; and (*b*) transformation rules, or rules
which explain how propositions can be transformed.
Typical of the first kind of rule are grammatical rules,
and typical of the second kind of rule are the laws of
inference which allow us to pass from one proposition
to another. Both kinds of rule are arbitrary, as is also
the vocabulary. This has long been recognized as regards grammatical rules, but it is only since the development of "alternative logics" that it has also been
recognized as regards the laws of inference. But if
these rules are arbitrary then it follows that to that
extent the truth of a proposition is man-made; and this
seems to me to be a sense, and a very important sense,
in which the Pragmatist statement is true.

But this is certainly not the sense in which the majority of Pragmatists maintain it to be true. Nor do
they maintain it to be true in the trivial sense that
when an individual alters something in the world,
then a proposition which was false before now becomes true. Rather they maintain that when an individual discovers in his own experience that a certain
proposition is true, then that individual has made the
proposition true. "Only that which has been organized
into our disposition so as to enable us to adapt the
environment to our needs and to adapt our aims and
desires to the situation in which we live is really
knowledge."[6] This naturally has important educational
consequences. "Thoughts just as thoughts are incomplete. At best they are tentative; they are suggestions,
indications. They are standpoints and methods for
dealing with situations of experience. Till they are

[5] Rudolf Carnap, *The Logical Syntax of Language* (London:
Routledge and K. Paul, 1937), p. 2.

[6] John Dewey, *Democracy and Education* (New York: Macmillan, 1916), p. 400.

applied in these situations they lack full point and
reality. Only application tests them, and only testing
confers full meaning and a sense of their reality."[7] It
is clear that this is merely a reformulation of one of
the propositions which Moore demolished—we can
verify all those of our ideas which are true—together
with the implication that it is our verification that
makes them true, which is just nonsense. I think it
must therefore be granted that the system commonly
known as Pragmatism is false in any of its ordinary
interpretations and, consequently, that it cannot be used
as an argument in support of any educational theory.
We have seen that one of the propositions generally
held to be implied by Pragmatism—our truths are
man-made products—is true, but the sense in which it
is true points to a method in education radically opposed to Dewey's. For it indicates, and Dewey denies,
that stress should be laid on what are traditionally
called the formal subjects—grammar and logic—as it
is only in so far as we use grammatical and logical
rules that we can be said to make a proposition true.

Dewey's acceptance of the doctrine of Pragmatism
has influenced his theory of education, particularly
with regard to the aim of education. It does not seem
to me that he has held the same view about the aim
of education throughout his life, and of course there
is no reason why he should. I shall, however, state
what I take to be his earlier view as well as what I take
to be his later view. I shall do this partly because I
am not quite certain that he has actually held the two
views, and if I state them both then there is a good
chance that he has actually held one of the views, and
partly because the earlier view has had great influence
among Dewey's followers.

The earlier view Dewey has expressed in this way.
"The radical error which child study would inhibit is,

[7] *Ibid.*, p. 189.

in my judgment, the habit of treating the child from
the standpoint of the teacher or parent; that is, considering the child as something to be educated, developed, instructed or amused. . . . The fundamental
principle is that the child is always a being with activities of his own which are present and urgent and do
not require to be 'induced,' 'drawn out,' 'developed'
etc., that the work of the educator, whether parent
or teacher, consists solely in ascertaining, and in con-
necting with, these activities, furnishing them appropriate opportunities and conditions."[8] Thus the child
must not be regarded as a "little man," and school life
must not be regarded as a training or preparation for
later life. But Dewey did hold that when these conditions were satisfied in school life then children would
be better suited to take part in adult social life. It is important to note that this result, successful participation in social life, was not put forward as an aim of
education, but was held to be a consequence of the
successful realization of the aim. Dewey has two arguments in favour of this view of education.

The first is as follows. Any society is a group of
people who have approximately the same interests
and who work for approximately the same aims. But
these characteristics do not apply to the traditional
school where there is no spontaneous common activity.
Therefore the traditional school is not a natural unit
of society. To make a school such a natural unit it is
necessary to consider what are the natural interests and
activities of the child and to organize the school with
the satisfaction of these as an aim. Hence there must
be radical differences from the traditional school, and
these differences are not merely differences in the
type of subject studied but differences in attitude.

[8] John Dewey, *Transactions of the Illinois Society for Child
Study,* Vol. I (January, 1895).

"We must conceive of work in wood and metal, of weaving, sewing and cooking as methods of living and learning, not as distinct studies. We must conceive of them in their social significance, as types of the processes by which society keeps itself going, as agencies for bringing home to the child some of the primal necessities of community life, and as ways in which these needs have been met by the growing insight and ingenuity of man; in short as instrumentalities through which the school itself shall be made a genuine form of active community life, instead of a place set apart in which to learn lessons."[9]

This argument does not justify Dewey's conclusions. It may be admitted that the traditional school is not a natural unit of society, but many educationists have held that the school ought not to be such a unit. It is at least logically possible that an extremely artificial schooling might be the best preparation for participation in social life later. Further I think it is probably because there was not a clear connexion between Dewey's aim and the effect of the realization of that aim on social life that Dewey did hold that aim and did not hold some social aim of education (although he did hold that, as a matter of fact, certain social consequences would follow from his aim).

The other argument in favour of this view of education is that it is consistent with the doctrine of Pragmatism. "No such thing as imposition of truth from without, as insertion of truth from without, is possible. All depends on the activity which the mind itself undergoes in responding to what is presented from without."[10] This is merely the same argument

[9] John Dewey, *The School and Society,* rev. ed. (Chicago: The University of Chicago Press, 1953), p. 11.

[10] John Dewey, *The Child and the Curriculum* (Chicago: The University of Chicago Press, 1902).

as was criticized at the beginning of the chapter. If an
idea is useful to a child then it is true, and unless it is
useful it is not true.

Although neither of these arguments affords any
justification for this view of education it is, nevertheless, possible that the view should be accepted.
It has been widely accepted and developed by some
of Dewey's disciples. A school organized on traditional
lines teaches a number of subjects—Mathematics, Languages, History, etc.—and its immediate aim is to
secure that its pupils attain efficiency in these subjects,
although some other aim may also be, and in general
is, held (such as the development of character). Some
theory is then necessary to explain, in some such way
as Herbart does, why knowledge of these subjects,
if it is attained, does lead to the achievement of this
further aim. It is true that such a theory is very often
taken for granted, and the success of a school is
judged by the extent to which it achieves its immediate aim. Now a school organized in accordance
with Dewey's aim does not teach a number of subjects. Kilpatrick, perhaps the most famous of Dewey's
followers, states that the guiding principle in the
organization is the bettering of the present life of
the child.[11] In order that this may be secured the following four rules[12] should be observed:

(1) The pupils must propose what they actually
do.

(2) They should be allowed to do only those things
which will build up certain attitudes.

(3) All learning should be done only if it is necessary for what the pupils have actually proposed.

(4) What the pupils are allowed to do should be

[11] Introduction to *An Experiment with a Project Curriculum,* by
Ellsworth Collings (New York: Macmillan, 1923), p. xvii.
[12] *Ibid.,* p. xvi.

guided so as to enrich "the subsequent stream of experience."

These are the bases of what is now generally called the project method of teaching. The children in consultation with the teacher propose some project. The teacher has power to veto any proposal, and selects the project which is most in accordance with rules 2 and 4. Other considerations also come in. The project must, for example, be practicable; that is, it must not involve apparatus impossible to make or to secure. The project must also be suitable to the age of the children and so on. The pupils then discuss plans for carrying out the project, and it is here that the teacher is probably of most help. The plans are then carried out and a report written which is criticized by the pupils and teachers.

Such a method of teaching must be carefully distinguished from the method often employed in traditional schools, namely, the method of utilizing the child's interests for teaching the various subjects. In the project method, the child's interests and purposes are the important thing, and the various subjects are regarded merely as means for satisfying these interests and purposes.

One minor criticism can be disposed of at once. It is clear that if the school is organized in accordance with these four rules, it is not true to say with Kilpatrick that the guiding principle is the bettering of the present life of the pupils. For both rules 2 and 4 involve reference to the future. It seems, therefore, that it would be better to give rules 1–4 as the principles guiding the organization (since these are the ones actually used), rather than some one general statement. Moreover, these are more consistent with Dewey's own position. "It will do harm if child study leave in the popular mind the impression that a child

of a given age has a positive equipment of purposes
and interests to be cultivated just as they stand. . . .
To take the phenomena presented at a given age as
in any way self-explanatory or self-contained is inevitably to result in indulgence and spoiling."[13]

But there are several serious criticisms which have
been advanced against the project method. The first
is that it is possible for the children not to acquire
certain types of knowledge if they do not propose
projects which are dependent on such knowledge.[14]
I think it is true that most of us are aware that a considerable part of our knowledge would not have been
acquired if we had been taught by the project method.
The project teacher may say that such knowledge
must be valueless and that instead we should have
obtained valuable knowledge, but I think a sufficient
answer to that is just that it is false.

A second criticism is that one of the well-known
laws of learning is violated. It is generally agreed that
if any skill is to be retained for any length of time,
then considerably more practice in it must be given
than is necessary for it just to be recalled. It is for
this reason that so much drill is given in the traditional
type of school for learning such things as the multi-
plication tables. But if all learning is to be done only
in so far as it is necessary for what the child has
proposed then there is no reason for giving drill. For
example, if a child is engaged in a problem which requires the solution of a quadratic equation then he
will be satisfied when he has been shown how to obtain
the solution. But it is absurd to imagine that he could
then solve another problem which depended on the
solution of a quadratic equation. Surely it is better
to adopt the customary procedure in text-books and

[13] Dewey, *op. cit.*
[14] G. H. Thomson, *A Modern Philosophy of Education* (London: G. Allen, 1929), p. 94.

to make the child work fifty or a hundred quadratic equations, after which he will be able to solve any problem of that type.

A third criticism is that the whole method assumes that the child has many interests and desires which it is the business of the educationist to satisfy, or according to the less extreme advocates, to guide. But interests and desires can be acquired as well as knowledge, and it seems almost obvious that many which are acquired in the traditional type of school are more valuable than those "naturally" occurring in the child. For example, an interest in Greek literature or in differential equations or in medieval history is often acquired, and it is surely the case that an interest in such a subject for its own sake is extremely valuable.

For these reasons it seems to me that the project method and the aim of education out of which the project method was developed must be considered inadequate. Dewey seems to have recognized this, for in his more recent writings he has advocated a somewhat different aim. I find his statement of this extremely difficult to follow and so, as far as possible, I shall let him speak for himself. "I take it that the fundamental unity of the newer philosophy is found in the idea that there is an intimate and necessary relation between the process of actual experience and education. . . . The problem for progressive education is: What is the place and meaning of subject matter and of organisation within experience?"[15] Continuing, Dewey says we need to know what experience is. "The belief that all genuine education comes about through experience does not mean that all experiences are genuinely or equally educative. Experience and education cannot be directly equated to each other. For some experiences are miseducative. Any experi-

[15] John Dewey, *Experience and Education* (New York: Macmillan, 1938), p. 7.

ence is miseducative that has the effect of arresting or
distorting the growth of further experience. An experience may be such as to engender callousness; it
may produce lack of sensitivity and of responsiveness.
Then the possibilities of having richer experience in
the future are restricted. Again a given experience
may increase a person's automatic skill in a particular
direction and yet tend to land him in a groove or rut;
the effect again is to narrow the field of further
experience."[16] The trouble with traditional education,
Dewey says, is not that the pupils do not have experiences but that they have the wrong kind of experience.
"Everything depends upon the *quality* of the experience which is had,"[17] and the quality of an experience
Dewey tells us is measured in two ways, first of all
by its immediate pleasantness or unpleasantness, and
secondly by its effect upon later experiences. "It is his
(the educationist's) business to arrange for the kind
of experiences which while they do not repel the
student, but rather engage his activities, are, nevertheless, more than immediately enjoyable since they
promote having desirable future experiences."[18]

These statements indicate that Dewey is paying less
attention to the immediate experiences and more attention to the future experiences of the pupil than
he did in his earlier statements about the aim of education. Nevertheless, they still seem to me unsatisfactory. The key word is the word "desirable," and as
everyone who has read John Stuart Mill knows there
are at least two meanings of "desirable" which it is
important to distinguish. For example, the sentence
"Beer is desirable in hot weather" means simply "Beer
is desired in hot weather." But the sentence "The
abolition of slums is desirable" means "The abolition

16 *Ibid.*, p. 13.
17 *Ibid.*, p. 16.
18 *Ibid.*, pp. 16–17.

of slums ought to be desired." That is, "the desirable"
may mean "what is desired" or "what ought to be
desired." If these meanings are substituted for "desirable" in Dewey's exposition we get the following two
statements:

(1) It is the educationist's business to arrange for
the kind of experiences which . . . are more than immediately enjoyable since they promote future experiences which are desired.

(2) It is the educationist's business to arrange for
the kind of experiences which . . . are more than
immediately enjoyable since they promote future experiences which ought to be desired.

Now the second statement might clearly be an account of the aim of a teacher in a traditional type of
school, and we must therefore conclude that it is
the first statement which expresses what Dewey actually means. But according to this statement the child
should have any experiences which will make it
easier for him to have the experiences he desires in
the future. Such a view would justify the training
of children to be gangsters or anything at all. It is, I
think, the confusion of the first statement with the
second which gives Dewey's theory its apparent plausi-
bility.

This later account of the aim of education is not
so pragmatic as the earlier, but it still seems to be
the acceptance of Pragmatism which prevents Dewey
asserting anything to be the end of the process of
education. He is continually preoccupied with the
guidance of present experience, and the direction of
the guidance is to be settled from day to day according to what is most useful. Indeed, Dewey's theory
of education may be regarded as the exact opposite
of the Jesuit theory. The latter was preoccupied with
the end of education and was not particular about the
means to reach the end. Dewey is preoccupied with

the means and is not particular what end he reaches.[19]

Perhaps I should also refer to another argument which Dewey gives in support of his type of school against the traditional. He urges that the traditional school is autocratic and that his type of school is democratic, and that democracy is inherently better than autocracy—better in the sense that "democratic social arrangements promote a better quality of human experience, one which is more widely accessible and enjoyed, than do non-democratic and anti-democratic forms of social life."[20] The validity of this argument depends, I think, on the assumption that the school can be isolated from the rest of the world. If everything outside the school were to remain exactly as it in fact is, then no doubt a democratic school would be better than an autocratic school. But clearly such an assumption is not true; and it may well be that an autocratic school is necessary to establish a democratic world. It is also doubtful, I think, whether the words "autocratic" and "democratic" can be used at all in their ordinary senses with reference to a school.

Dewey's pragmatic views have also influenced his conception of the Laboratory School—the name which he gave to a school which he founded while he was at the University of Chicago. His intention was that this school should have the same relation to the Department of Philosophy, Psychology and Education as a scientific laboratory has to the branch of science associated with it. Now the use of a scientific laboratory is (1) to obtain knowledge of facts and laws hitherto unknown, and (2) to test scientific theories by the invention of crucial experiments. Hence we may say that the purpose of the Laboratory School was (1) to obtain knowledge of facts and laws hitherto un-

---

[19] I need hardly warn the reader that this, taken literally, is grossly unfair to both the Jesuits and Dewey.

[20] Dewey, *Experience and Education*, p. 25.

known to educationists, and (2) to test educational theories by the invention of crucial experiments.

Perhaps I should explain what is meant by a crucial experiment. Suppose a number of facts have been observed. Then it is possible to construct many theories all of which will explain the observed facts, and the problem arises as to which of these theories is to be accepted. The recognized scientific procedure is to attempt to deduce theoretically some consequence for each theory which is not implied by any other theory, and then to investigate experimentally which of these consequences is verified. For example, when the observed facts were the motions of the planets of the solar system, it was found possible to construct both the Newtonian and Einsteinian gravitational theories to explain them. Also from Einstein's theory it followed that light should be deflected as it passed through the sun's gravitational field, while from Newton's theory it did not follow. By experiment, however, it was found that such a consequence did take place, and therefore Einstein's theory superseded Newton's. Such an experiment as verifying the deflexion of light in the sun's gravitational field is called a crucial experiment.

If the records of the Laboratory School are examined, however, it becomes clear that the parallel with a scientific laboratory breaks down. It is certainly possible to obtain knowledge of facts hitherto unknown, and from these it may be possible to obtain by induction knowledge of laws hitherto unknown. But it is quite impossible to test educational theories by means of crucial experiments in a Laboratory School. For most educational theories involve some reference to after-school life. Before such a theory could be either confirmed or refuted it would therefore be necessary for knowledge to be obtained not only about the facts of school life but also about the facts of later life, and

about the way in which these are connected with the
facts of school life. That is, if an educational theory
has reference to what happens in after-school life,
then it can be neither confirmed nor refuted by appeal to what happens in school only. Hence the
Laboratory School can at best fulfill only the first
function of a scientific laboratory. This first function of a scientific laboratory—the discovery of hitherto unknown facts—has nothing to do with the
verification of theories, and all educationists, whatever the theories they hold, would agree that there
should exist schools in which new facts and laws could
be discovered. Thus Dewey's conception of the Laboratory School is valuable in so far as the school is
not considered to be a place where educational theories
are verified and refuted; and it seems to me probable
that Dewey would not have regarded it in this second light if he had not been so obsessed by the idea
of verification, which in turn was due to his acceptance of Pragmatism.

RELEVANT READING

Dewey, John, "The Nature of Method," *Democracy and Edu-
    cation*. New York: The Macmillan Company, 1916.
—— *Reconstruction in Philosophy*. Boston: The Beacon Press,
    1948.
—— "The Construction of Good," *The Quest for Certainty*.
    New York: Minton, Balch & Co., 1929.
—— *The Sources of a Science of Education*. New York:
    Horace Liveright, 1929.
—— *How We Think*. Boston: D. C. Heath & Company, 1933.
—— *Experience and Education*. New York: The Macmillan
    Company, 1939.
Hardie, Charles D., "The Philosophy of Education in a New
    Key." *Educational Theory*, X (October, 1960).
Hill, Walker H., "Peirce and Pragmatism." *Journal of Philoso-
    phy*, XXXVI (December 7, 1939).
James, William, *Pragmatism, A New Name for Some Old*

Ways of Thinking. New York: Longmans, Green & Company, 1907.

Kilpatrick, William H., *Foundations of Method*. New York: The Macmillan Company, 1925.

Mayhew, Katherine C., and Edwards, Anna C., *The Dewey School: The Laboratory School of the University of Chicago 1896–1903*. New York: D. Appleton-Century Company, 1936.

John Dewey: His Philosophy of Education and Its Critics

❀

Sidney Hook

On the 100th anniversary of his birth and but seven years after his death, the educational philosophy of John Dewey stands condemned by the highest political authority in the United States. In a letter published in *Life* (March 15, 1959), President Eisenhower, who also served briefly as President of Columbia University, where John Dewey taught for more than a quarter-century, wrote: "Educators, parents and students must be continuously stirred up by the defects in our educational system. They must be induced to abandon the educational path that, rather blindly, they have been following as a result of John Dewey's teachings."

This criticism climaxes the offensive from different quarters of the ideological compass against Dewey's

This selection originally appeared as a supplement to *The New Leader*, November, 1959. Mr. Hook is Professor of Philosophy at New York University.

educational philosophy. Book upon book, article upon
article develops the same theme. Criticism of the
multiple inadequacies of American education is coupled
with large, vague but forthright attacks on John Dewey
as the prime cause of American failure. Even the
Navy and Marines have been called in! One of the
most strident books in this vein is Vice Admiral Hyman
Rickover's *Education and Freedom,* which should
properly be entitled "Education for Victory in the
Next War." It is both striking and significant that
most of the criticism does not even attempt to come to
grips with Dewey's central educational doctrines. Instead, it merely deplores the faults and weaknesses of
American education—in the light of the threat to freedom's future implicit in Soviet technological advance.

For all their legitimate, if newly awakened, concern with education today, one gets the impression that
the most vocal latter-day critics do not themselves
exhibit that value of *conscientiousness* in their criticism
which they would have our schools stress in their
curriculum. They seem to be looking for a scapegoat
for our predicament rather than for its genuine causes.
If they had actually read Dewey instead of denounc-
ing him, they would have observed that he himself
was a lifelong critic of American education, and that
on occasion his criticism extended even to that small
private sector of American education which was "progressive" in orientation and took its point of departure
from his principles. More important still, it was John
Dewey who long ago foresaw and warned against
the very elements which have produced the crisis
of our times and set off the current hysteria about
the state of American education.

It is generally agreed that the main outlines of our
crisis were shaped by the convergence of two great
phenomena. The first is the transformative effects of
science and technology on society, industry and cul-

ture. The second is the emergence of Communist totalitarianism as an expanding imperialism which sees in the United States the chief foe to its crusade for world domination.

During the last 50 years of his life, Dewey defined our age as the age of the scientific revolution. He called upon educators to take note of the vast implications of the scientific revolution, of the changes it produced in our way of life. He urged a searching inquiry into the institutions, principles and methods necessary to channel and master these changes in the interest of inclusive and humane ends. Calling for improvement of science instruction in elementary schools more than a half-century ago, he wrote: "I believe the attitude toward the study of science is, and should be, fixed during the earlier years." He took scientific knowledge as his paradigm of knowledge; and he proposed that its basic *logic* or *pattern* of thinking, as distinct from specific techniques and methods, be adopted as a norm in thinking wisely about political and social affairs. Some of the critics who have joined the outcry that Dewey has ill-prepared American schools for the challenge of our scientific and technological world are the very ones who not long ago charged him with "scientism," with placing undue emphasis upon the mode of scientific experience while slighting other modes. The simple truth is that no one who took Dewey's educational ideas seriously would have been surprised by recent technological advances.

The same is true for the other major explosive element in the current situation. During the last 20 years of his life, and most especially during World War II when the Soviet Union was being hailed by professional humanists and scientists, by leading admirals and generals and politicians, as a trusted ally of the democratic powers, Dewey described the nature of the

Communist threat to the free world. He did not wait
for the Kremlin to put a satellite in the sky to recognize the portents of disaster. He proclaimed them when
the Kremlin established its satellites on earth—and even
before then. He called for an intelligent foreign policy
based on realistic understanding of the nature of Communism, which he had studied intensively from the
time of the infamous Moscow Trials in the mid-'30s.

It is the absence of this intelligent foreign policy,
for which the politicians, generals and admirals are
chiefly responsible, that accounts for the particular
crisis today that agitates Admiral Rickover and his
confreres. During the last war, the American educational system was no better and in some respects it
was much worse than it is today. But we had enough
political gumption to realize what the nature of Hitler-
ism was—and what its victory would mean to the
prospects of freedom. We were able to introduce the
emergency research programs which insured our victory.

What happened subsequently? Those responsible for
political and defense policy failed to understand the
nature of Communism and failed, therefore, to provide the leadership and vision required to contain the
newer and more dangerous threat to freedom. They
stumbled from error to error, from one improvisation
to another, from appeasement to bluster. They were
unable to take the initiative with intelligent policies
because they lacked a clear grasp of nationalism, of
Communism, and of the impact of the new scientific
revolution upon the world.

I should not like to be misunderstood as implying
that failures and successes in foreign policy flow *directly* from educational philosophy or practice. But
precisely such a proposition seems to be implied by the
grand panjandrums of the anti-Dewey parade who are
convulsed with fury at what they call progressive edu-

cation. For what they really are deploring is our truly serious condition *vis-à-vis* the growing power of the totalitarian world—a serious condition that testifies to the defect of political intelligence, and sometimes of elementary political knowledge, on the part of those responsible for that policy in the past. If education is relevant to this question, we must look to the education of those in strategic places and command posts. Have those who have neglected the needs of scientific military defense from Pearl Harbor to the present, who have systematically neglected the opportunities for democratic ideological warfare, who have failed to make the United States the leader of the world movement for colonial liberation—have all those politicians, generals and admirals been brought up on progressive education, or in the spirit of Dewey's educational philosophy?

Admiral Rickover and some Dewey critics seem to be interested in an education which will help us win the next war. If Dewey's educational philosophy had truly guided American education and inspired the architects of American foreign policy, their concern would have been how to avoid a world war and yet preserve and extend the heritage of free society. For this is a corollary of the basic educational aim of Dewey's philosophy—education for creative intelligence in a world of peace and freedom and *danger*.

Despite those who tax him with lapsing into a cheerful and complacent naturalism because man is "in" and "of" nature, the world as it struck Dewey has at least two outstanding traits. It is a world of danger —which fluctuates in intensity, but is always present— and it is a world of opportunity. The dangers are more obvious than the opportunities because most of the time the opportunities have to be sought for, they have to be made or discovered. In a precarious world, thinking diminishes danger by enlarging opportunity.

An education which equips man to live a significant life in a dangerous world cannot be the "soft education" which the Rickovers properly decry. Nor must it necessarily be the "hard education" of technical, mathematical and scientific courses which they currently are crying up. The world may be dangerous not only because of our ignorance of advanced mathematics and physics, but because of our ignorance of elementary politics, economics and social psychology. Without genuine *political* understanding, the leaders of the Western world could not prevent Communism's postwar expansion, even if they possessed the mathematical and scientific knowledge of an Einstein.

THREE CENTRAL IDEAS

I shall present briefly three leading ideas which seem to me central to Dewey's philosophy of education. They are his theory of experience, his conception of democracy, and his emphasis on scientific method in education.

The term "experience" has many different meanings, but the sense which Dewey gives it makes it relevant to the human learning process. All education is occasioned by experience, but for Dewey not all experiences are genuinely educational. He regards only those experiences to which the individual reacts with an informed awareness of the problems and challenge of his environment as truly educational. Such a reaction increases our actual or potential power of control in relation to environment or self. For all his naturalism, Dewey is post-Kantian in his theory of experience. Human beings do not merely endure or suffer events or happenings, they actively experience them. To experience them is to take them in a certain way, to react in a manner which expresses the total state of the organism and reflects the cultural and historical situations in which that organism has developed.

To the extent that the organism is passive, it may be trained to react by automatic drill and other forms of conditioning, but no genuine human learning occurs as distinct from animal learning. Some element of activity, of attending and therefore selecting, must be present. Even reading, which seems to take place by passive absorption, cannot give understanding unless the mind reaches out, so to speak, to grasp the sense of the passage. The intercepted light signals and the retinal images are not enough. The meaning and significant content of an experience depend precisely upon this grasp or outreaching of the mind, which responds to, relates and interrelates the elements of the experience.

Dewey's theory of experience is not derived from arbitrary philosophical premises but from modern psychology. In many ways, experimental findings confirm his view that even what a man observes cannot be adequately accounted for without reference to the active role of the observer, his history and cultural context. As Adelbert Ames and others have shown, perception is not merely a mirroring of what is given but the consequence of some interaction—or better still, a transaction between organism and environment, self and not self. It is this theory of experience which underlies Dewey's conception of man as a creature who, although bound by the antecedent conditions of his existence, can within limits redirect and redetermine both the world and himself and become morally responsible for those things which his thought and action can influence.

All this, Dewey would say, is descriptive of what experience is and how we learn by and through experience. But Dewey has a normative approach to what the educational experience should be. He distinguishes between two aspects of an experience, its *impact* and its *effect*. Its impact is the felt immediacy of being exciting or boring, agreeable or disagreeable, pleasurable or painful. The active response in this aspect of experience is of short range. It is atomic or pulselike and dies with the occasion. The second aspect is its effect upon further experiences. This effect may be measured by the extent to which the learner sees meaning in his present experience, reacts to its possible leads and interpretations, and thus prepares himself to understand better, and to some degree control, future experience.

This is why, for Dewey, "the central problem of an education based upon experience is to select the kind of present experiences that live fruitfully and creatively in subsequent experiences." To do this a whole series of selections is necessary which result not merely in organized subject matter but a certain kind of subject matter, not merely in discipline but a certain kind of discipline, not merely in method of instruction but a certain kind of method. But they all have two things in common.

First, they are selected with an eye to the continuity of experience, or, more accurately, to the expected continuities of experience, so that future experiences become more readily accessible to us on the basis of our past experience. This does not mean neglect of subject matter but the proper organization of subject matter. And it does not mean that all subject matters are equally important. "The curriculum must be planned with reference to essentials first, and refinements second." What is essential depends on a number of variables. Second, subject matters, methods and discipline are to be selected so as to maximize the active participation of the learner in the process of learning. This stress upon the element of activity in educa-

tional experience is congenial to Dewey's interpretation of "ideas" as implicit plans of action or operations
to be carried out in appropriate situations; of "understanding" as congruous and conjoint behavior in
partaking in a common enterprise; of "truth" as warranted assertion emerging from the transformative
activities of experiment; and of "intelligence" as creative thinking which by sign-using behavior alters situations in such a way as to resolve their problematic
character.

Whether these interpretations of "ideas," "truth,"
"understanding" and "intelligence" are valid I shall
not discuss here. Like all other interpretations they
have their difficulties. But I stress the character of
these interpretations and of Dewey's theory of experience because it enables us to assess some of the criticisms of Dewey's philosophy of education.

I am referring particularly to the view that Dewey
emphasizes adjustment to society—if not to present
society, then to some future society. Admiral Rickover
writes: "The American people have never authorized
the schools to replace education with life-adjustment
training and behavioral conditioning. Yet we have
permitted the schools to experiment with Dewey's
ideas for a long time."

Can misunderstanding be more complete? It would
be a more legitimate, even if mistaken, criticism of
Dewey to say that the development of intelligence
is more likely to lead to estrangement from society
or opposition to it or a desire to reform and transform
it. In order to be intelligent one must have ideas. To
have ideas is to be committed or ready to act on them.
To act on them means introducing a directed change
either in the environment or ourselves. According to
Dewey, we make our environment in part because our
response to it is a selective response depending upon
our attention and interest. We make our environment

only in part because we must accept most of it without thinking—thinking is done only on occasion—and because the results of all sane thinking must acknowledge the existence of what exercises compulsion upon what we do. But the world we live in, whether personal or public, private or shared, to the extent that we act intelligently in it, is *partly* of our creation. That is why we are responsible for those features of it that could be different were we to think and act otherwise.

The only person who is adjusted to his environment in the mindless way Admiral Rickover implies is one in a state of torpor, inattention, absence of interest, boredom. To be awake and alive in a world where problems exist means to be alarmed, on guard, ready to do something in relation to what is about to be or about to happen. Ironically, the pejorative educational connotations of "adjustment" may be most legitimately applied to the conception held by some of Dewey's critics.

In one of these connotations, adjustment suggests subordination to the *status quo*, not merely learning *about* the conditions of life, but compliance to its norms. The "adjusted" individual assimilates social use and wont, the traditional ways of action, to the compulsions of natural necessity. In the past, education for this type of adjustment was associated with drill, habitual obedience, automatic response, the performance of set tasks under set conditions, the assumption that there is usually only one right way of doing anything and that some person in authority must ultimately define it. This kind of education is more reminiscent of traditional military training than of modern education.

An allied notion of "adjustment" is involved in views which regard the function of education to be the "pouring" or "cramming" of subject matter—honor-

ifically labelled "the great traditions of the past"—
into the students' minds, as if they were inert recep-
tacles or containers to be filled rather than powers to
be stirred and developed. Such an approach fails to
give students a sense of *why* subject matters matter.
It also fails to make ideas, people and events come alive
in the direct or imaginative experience of those who
are learning.

All of these conceptions of adjustment or *self*-
adjustment are foreign to Dewey's educational philosophy. For they do not envisage the adjustment of
society to the moral imperatives of educational growth.
Nor do they adjust the curriculum to the needs and
capacities of students in order to achieve maximum
educational growth. A curriculum designed and taught
in the light of Dewey's philosophy seeks to quicken
powers of perception, wherever relevant, into how
things have become what they are; into how they
may become better or worse; and into what our responsibility, personal or social, is for making them better or worse. It strives to make the student sensitive
to the kind of problems he will have to meet in wider
contexts when he is through with formal schooling.
It is not romantic or utopian. Although it liberates
the mind by opening visions of alternatives, it curbs
the will and disciplines the imagination by recognizing
that not all alternatives are possible or equally probable. Certain objective conditions must be learned and
accepted in order to introduce intelligent changes.
No one can be wise who is not resigned about something, or who tries to dissolve the stubborn facts in
the rose water of myth or hope. But wherever conditions impinge upon men, men can also impinge upon
conditions. One can adjust to the weather by letting
oneself be rained on or by learning to keep dry in the
rain. What is true of weather is true of everything
else that is meaningfully perceived in life—even death.

So long as one remains conscious, one can determine something important about his own death. We can die like jackals or like men.

Terms like "adjustment" or "non-adjustment," like the terms "conformism" or "non-conformism," are essentially relational. Used without reference to a context, as most critics employ them, they are meaningless. Unless we know *what* is being adjusted to and *how*, what is being conformed to or not, these terms have merely emotive overtones but no cognitive significance. When the context and use are supplied, the only kind of adjustment Dewey would approve of is that which develops independent or creative intelligence.

INTELLIGENCE VS. TRADITION

I do not mean to imply that all criticisms of Dewey's theory of experience are of the same uninformed character as those considered above. His theory of experience is primarily an empirical hypothesis to explain psychological data. Ultimately, its formulations must be tested by observation and clarified by analysis. Its bearing on the philosophy of education is apparent when we consider the ends and methods of education. Certain ends are to be ruled out if, because they run counter to the normal course of experience, they exact too great a price in needless frustration, friction or pain. But it is possible on the basis of the same theory of experience, Dewey's or any other, to defend different educational ends. At this point we move from the plane of psychology to ethics and social philosophy. An analogy may make this clearer: Certain methods of teaching reading may be ruled out as undesirable because of what we know about the biology and psychology of vision. But even where we agree about the best methods of teaching reading, this by itself will not determine the content of reading or what *should be* read.

Nonetheless, I must confess myself puzzled to understand, in the light of Dewey's own writings, many of the criticisms made by some well-meaning and otherwise well-informed critics of his theory of experience. For example, Professor I. B. Berkson interprets Dewey and the experimentalists generally as meaning by "experience" only biological and social processes of interaction and excluding ethical and ideal moments. As if the social components of experience are not already drenched with ethical attitudes and values!

This is bound up with the kindred criticism that, because of their attack on fixed assumptions, Dewey and the experimentalists "leave the impression that we can derive conclusions from direct experience without making any assumptions" (Berkson, *The Ideal and the Community*, Harper). This would make Dewey sin against the very first principles of his own theory of inquiry. For him an open mind is not an empty mind. Doubt arises not because we are ignorant but because what we assume to be true doesn't appear to be so. The view that for Dewey thinking starts from scratch and that any subject matter, especially *historical* subject matter, is to be approached with a mind born yesterday is simply quaint. It is a caricature even of 18th century rationalism.

It is a commonplace of the experimental tradition that, as Charles Peirce put it, we cannot doubt all things at once. And it is a simple fact of experience that men and especially children suffer not from an excess of doubt but of credulity and dogmatism. This explains the experimentalist's emphasis not on the absence of presuppositions and assumptions—some-

thing must always be taken for granted—but on the
importance of developing habits of inquiry as we
begin to learn, and the growing importance of these
habits of inquiry as the student grows older. As
Dewey said in *Experience and Nature*, "What is already known, what is accepted as truth, is of immense
importance; inquiry could not proceed a step without it."

The criticism that experimentalism places such emphasis upon primary and immediate experience as
to exclude tradition, a sense of history and of the
past from learning is a recurrent theme of many different schools of critics. This is evident even when they
quote Dewey to the effect that "ours is the responsibility of conserving, transmitting, rectifying and expanding the heritage of values we have received that
those who come after us may receive it more solid and
secure, more widely accessible, and more generously
shared than we have received it." I am convinced that
this kind of criticism is based upon a totally naive view
of history and an unjustified fear that when we study
the present intelligently we can never escape reference
to history.

Test this criticism by an illustration. Nothing is more
topical than the issue of integration in Little Rock.
No social studies teacher can ignore it as part of relevant subject matter. But who could discuss it intelligently without reference to *historical* factors in
politics, law, economics, and ethics? The entire texture
of social and cultural subject matter is woven out of
historical strands—some short, some long, but all so
inextricably and intricately intertwined that we need
some principle of relevance to snip their connections
to understand what bears on the present. And how can
Little Rock be evaluated without some defensible
commitment to an ideal of democracy, freedom and

fair play; to some conception of federal, states and individual rights; to rule by majorities, absolute or concurrent, and their relation to minorities? But just as soon as we seek to ground these commitments in history we find that history is not enough. There are many histories, and our selection of guides from among them, Jefferson or Hamilton, Lincoln or Calhoun, Wilson or Debs, expresses in the last analysis a moral judgment which we must show to be viable in the present. We cannot escape the primacy of history when social fact is considered. Nor can we escape the primacy of morality where social policy is considered.

What then is the issue? The issue, I make bold to say, is whether we are to accept uncritical history—a traditionalism which under the guise of respect for tradition smuggles in bias and prejudice—or whether we are to accept an approach to history which gives loyalty to truth or the methods of discovering the truth where knowledge of the past is concerned. Dewey would agree with Pascal's statement—although not with his reasons for saying it—that "whatever right antiquity may claim, truth always has a prior claim, no matter how new its discovery."

What, for example, is suggested in the following passage from Berkson's *The Ideal and the Community:* "More is lost than gained when the regime of purposeful activity and critical intelligence is represented as a substitute for, instead of as a supplement to, instilling a devotion to principles and directing toward definite moral ends. The undertone of antagonism to authority, to traditional belief, to doing right for right's sake is likely to lead to loosening of existing standards rather than raising to a higher mode of conduct. In its lack of confidence in the established order, experimentalism unwittingly casts a shadow of distrust on

conventional mores and accepted institutional forms
even when these serve valid social purposes." (Italics
mine.)

To me, this suggests the perennial complaint of the
traditionalist and fearful conservative against the cor-
rosive effects of intelligence. Experimentalism is de-
cried because it raises doubts about conventional forms
"*even when these serve valid social purposes.*" But if
they *do* serve valid social purposes, why should critical
intelligence sustain doubt? The very language of the
passage quoted could just as easily be employed by
Prussian schoolteachers and Southern Bourbons convinced that existing institutions serve valid social purposes—and a liberal like Berkson would be among the
first to disavow them.

Nonetheless, the assumption of the passage is that
children come to school doubting Thomases from
homes in which they have been nurtured by a religion
of Critical Reason equipped with dialectical weapons.
But every teacher knows that they come with the
prejudices of their communities prepared to believe
whatever they are told, intolerant even of differences
in dress, speech, manner and thought. One would think
that juvenile delinquency is the consequence of hyper-
critical intelligence! The causes of juvenile delinquency
are many and what takes place in the schools has pre-
cious little to do with them. But to the extent that there
is some connection, one can more plausibly argue that
the failure of the school to demonstrate the valid social purposes of existing laws and institutions and to
bring home a vivid, imaginative and convincing sense
of their justifications, makes it easier for students to disregard them.

"Not all who say *Ideals, Ideals,*" Dewey reminds us
in "The Pragmatic Acquiescence," "shall enter the
kingdom of the ideal, but only those shall enter who
know and who respect the roads that conduct to the

kingdom." The roads which are to conduct us to the kingdom of the ideal must be built by the best methods of intelligence (or reason or scientific inquiry) available to us. And whether or not we ultimately reach the kingdom is not so important as the direction in which we move and how we move. Agreement on goals and ideals means little in practice unless we can agree on methods and procedures of reaching them. At the risk of being misunderstood, I say that there is greater difference among those who proclaim their agreement about goals and disagree about methods, means and procedures, than there is among those who agree upon the latter and leave open the question of whether they further agree upon "ultimate" ends—if there are such. Every "ultimate end" in a concrete historical context is analyzable into a "penultimate end." For Dewey, just as use of different means results in different ends, so different roads lead to different kingdoms.

What is true of the place of history in education is also true of the place of subject matter and the function of the teacher. There is absolutely nothing in Dewey's theory of experience and education which makes the subject matter and/or the teacher dispensable. The misconceptions about this derive from a misunderstanding of, and sometimes disagreement with, Dewey's conception of democracy in education. To this I now turn.

DEMOCRACY IN EDUCATION

Dewey's philosophy of education, as everyone knows, makes central democracy in education. Although the phrase "democracy in education" has become a shibboleth, so that few will openly declare that they oppose it, it has many different meanings. It is commonly assumed that Dewey's conception of democracy in education encourages, if it does not entail, the cult of me-

diocrity, and the systematic denigration of intellectual
excellence. To assess the validity of this charge, it is
necessary to examine with some care what Dewey
means both by democracy and by democracy in education.

Democracy in most contexts refers to a form of government or political process by which those who rule
are elected by the freely given consent of a majority of
the adults governed. Although Dewey was a democrat
in this sense, he did not regard democracy or any other
political process or institution as an end in itself. He
realized that a democracy could function poorly and
that it was capable of acting abominably, *e.g.*, in its
treatment of minorities in the South or elsewhere. All
his life he criticized the functioning of American democracy in the light of a more basic conception of
democracy which he called "moral and ideal."

The essence of Dewey's view was that democracy
was committed to an equality of concern for each individual in the community to develop himself as a
person. Education was the chief means by which those
personal capacities were to be discovered and liberated.
Education would enable human beings to achieve their
maximum *distinctive* growth in harmony with their
fellows. Equality of concern is not the same thing as
equal treatment. It is compatible with unequal treatment, provided this treatmnt is required by the necessities of intellectual and emotional growth in each case.
"Moral equality," he says, "means incommensurability,
the inapplicability of common and quantitative standards. It means intrinsic qualities which require *unique*
opportunities and *differential* manifestation. . . ." The
principle of moral equality or ideal democracy is the
most revolutionary principle in the world because its
scope embraces all social institutions.

Any honest reading of Dewey indicates that individuals come first in the order of concern, and that to be

an individual is to be different in some distinctive and important way even though many things are shared in common with others. Conceptually, it is very difficult to express this union of equality of concern and difference of treatment in a formal rule. But we may illustrate it by reference to another institution: In a healthy and happy family where children vary in age, strength and intellectual gifts, it would be absurd for parents to treat them equally—absurd precisely because they are considered equal, valued equally. A family, of course, cannot be taken as a model for a complex society—there are no parents in society—but ethically it illustrates the principle which Dewey believed should be exhibited in the functioning of social institutions in a democracy, or which should be its controlling and guiding spirit. And it is striking to observe how often Dewey uses the family for analogical purposes to make an educational recommendation. For example, his well-known words: "What the best and wisest parent wants for his own child, that must the community want for all its children. Any other ideal for our schools is narrow and unlovely; acted upon, it destroys our democracy."

The significance of this observation is all the more important as an indicator of Dewey's meaning, because the words are such an obvious overstatement. We have never acted on this ideal and have not destroyed our democracy, because democracy so conceived has never really existed. But these words do express in the most emphatic way an entire complex of values, values which must guide our action if we are to approach closer to the democratic ideal. And this ideal rests on the primacy of freedom, on the right to be different, on the right to be an individual—so much so that, although social institutions are recognized as the indispensable means by which personality is aided in coming to development, all social institutions must nevertheless be criticized and reformed in the light of the qualities of human experience to which they give rise. The individual person comes first in the order of significance, not of time.

The educational corollaries which follow from such a democratic philosophy are fantastically different from those drawn by critics who see in it the prolegomenon to an ideological justification for mediocrity. The very contrary is true. Mediocrity is the consequence of imposing one uniform pattern on individual differences, of the attempt to make everyone talk and sing and think alike about the same things at the same time. How can Dewey's philosophy be interpreted as advocating that the gifted child be denied the special attention which would bring his gifts to fruition? Historically, the earliest concern with providing appropriate educational opportunities for gifted children was manifested by educators and psychologists strongly influenced by Dewey. By all means, education must aim at excellence! But is there only one kind of excellence? Must one excellence be sacrificed to another? Must, as Ernest Renan asks, whatever is unfit for the altar of the gods be thrown to the dogs? Or, put more concretely, does it follow that, because we should exert our efforts to provide the educational stimulation that will generate the most fruitful results for students of the highest IQ, we should therefore not exert ourselves to generate the most fruitful results for students of lower IQs? If this is what it means, where is our equality of concern?

We must distinguish between standards of achievement that individuals must measure up to before certain professions are open to them—and from which, both in their own personal interests and those of society, they can be legitimately barred—and the standard of growth and progress that is applicable to each individual. It is the latter which concerns the teacher, insofar as he accepts responsibility for the education of the person. And this means not the elimination or the dilution of subject matter, not the substitution of play for study, not a cafeteria of snap courses—but holding up ever higher goals to be reached by every student until he has attained *his* best. Such an approach is perfectly compatible with prescribed courses and studies. For if all needs are individual, many of them are at the same time common needs in a common world of common dangers and opportunities. There are some things everyone needs to know, but not everything needs to be known by everybody.

What this democratic conception of education involves is better grasped by contrasting it with the view that would not merely discriminate *between* capacities but *against* them. Such a view advocates a kind of elite system in which the prizes and the power go to those who by natural endowment or social preferment (the two are often hard to separate) reach the head of their class. It not only differentiates but subtly demeans by suggesting that the hierarchy of intelligence is the key to the hierarchy of human value, which sooner or later determines position in a hierarchy of social standing and political power. Sometimes this view also calls itself democratic, but its spirit as well as its recommendations are altogether opposed to democracy as Dewey understood it.

Let us examine, for example, the view of Professor William Hocking, who has written widely on education. For him genuine democracy consists in *"the democracy of identical standard"* to be applied to all, irrespective of capacities. And he explains his meaning by an analogy: "We do not, in our athletic contests, trim the length of the mile to the convenience of the runners. The democracy of the race does not consist in the assumption that everybody must get a prize; it consists in the identity of the spacing and timing for

all entrants. This is what democracy must mean in
higher education, and to retain this integrity, there
must be losers, and a thinning out of the mass trend
to the colleges" (*Experiment in Education*, Regnery,
1954). What this means in practice is indicated by the
question: "But where is the college which is willing
to flunk 50 per cent of its graduating class?"

Hocking does not explain why democracy means
this only in higher education and not in secondary or
even primary education. If "every man has a right and
duty to be a whole man," as he puts it, why has not
every individual a right to that kind of education
which will carry him further to that wholeness at any
level? And what has all this to do with degrees or
certification of professional competence, which are
fundamentally socially protective devices? And above
all, what has the process of education to do with a race?
And even in a race, we do not expect, unless we are
Nietzschean, the halt, the blind, the crippled to start
from scratch. And if the course of study is to be considered like a race course, who ever heard of 50 per
cent of the runners winning the prize? Why not flunk
90 per cent of the graduating class—indeed, why not
all except the man who wins by coming in first?

The analogy reveals the unconscious, anti-democratic, almost Prussian, conception underlying this view
of education. Education is not a race or combat or
a competition, although, properly implemented, these
may be pedagogic devices to add zest to learning. If we
prefer to use language of this sort, it is better to have
the individual run a race against his own potentialities,
which, since they grow with achievement, means that
the race, like the process of education and self-educa-
tion, is never finished.

Allied to this conception of education as the process
by which prizes and power are won is the view of

society as a graded and hierarchically organized society, in which intelligence, not birth, social status or wealth, is the principle of differentiation. No matter what the principle of differentiation is, if it involves hierarchy, official or unofficial, it involves the likelihood of exploitation. It is well to realize that we do not owe the great movements for social justice and political freedom to the educated classes of hierarchically ordered European societies. On the whole, they sided with church and king and the social *status quo* during the centuries of struggle for the extension of human rights. Higher intelligence and specialized education give both the duty and right to exercise specific functions in a complex society, but so does not-so-high intelligence and more general education. Unless there is a mutuality of esteem and a recognition that there are many kinds of desirable distinctions, the entire principle of distinction becomes invidious, a badge of social snobbery and an instrument by which special interests are furthered. A society in which there are class struggles between the better educated and the less well educated, between the more intelligent and the less intelligent, not only violates the principles of moral equality, but is one in which the best educated are likely to lose.

There is another aspect of democracy in education which is intimately connected with modern American education. It has been travestied and caricatured not only by critics, but by some unintelligent followers of Dewey. This is the view that at appropriate levels the student's educational experience—his group meetings, school projects, class organization—exhibits some of the values which are central to the ethics of democracy. In a country of different races and varied ethnic groups in which the family itself may be the original breeding place of violent prejudice, such activities are all the

more necessary. Whatever "character education" is,
it is more likely to take by being lived than by being
preached. Where students are made responsible for
some aspects of their school life, this need not interfere either with the time devoted to learning or with
the seriousness with which it is prosecuted. A skilful
teacher can so organize instruction that often the
educational lesson or project draws all children into
it in some participating role for which they take
responsibility.

The easiest way to make this idea ridiculous is to try
to carry it out with young toughs or hooligans produced by the breakdown of family and community
life in large cities—especially where there has been
a recent influx of immigrants. A pinch of common
sense is sometimes better than a carload of speculative
pedagogy. Although Dewey never realized the extent
and gravity of the problem, he did recognize that in
the case of disturbed and unruly students who "stand
permanently in the way of the educational activities
of others . . . exclusion is perhaps the *only* available
measure at a given juncture, even though it is no
solution." (Italics mine.)

Every classroom teacher knows that it requires only
one or two such students to make genuine teaching
impossible. Nonetheless, the community—or rather,
newspapers and educational pressure groups which
decry modern education—cites the existence of such
elements (which in the past either did not get to
school or received short shrift when they did) as evidence of the failure of modern education. Nothing in
Dewey's or anybody else's educational philosophy
requires the schools to function like psychiatric and/or
police institutions. Something should and can be done
for such students—a democratic society should be
equally concerned about them, too, but they must be
firmly excluded for their sake and the sake of other

children from the normal school environment until they are rehabilitated.

ANTI-SCIENTIFIC DOGMATISM

Some of Dewey's distinctive views on education do not follow from his general pragmatic philosophy. On the contrary, he developed the latter, in part, on the basis of his reflection on, and observation of, those processes of education which seemed to succeed best in teaching students to acquire certain desirable skills, habits, values and knowledge of subject matter. Dewey held the distinctive view that the scientific psychological study of the ways human beings learn, of the effects of individual differences on learning, of the interrelation of interest, insight and effort, gives us more reliable knowledge than the anecdotal methods of uncritical common sense. He held that we should use this knowledge in devising and testing teaching methods. If we wish to teach reading or any other subject worth teaching, there is a bad and a good and a better way of teaching it; there is an appropriate and an inappropriate time for teaching it, in order to get the best results; above all, there is a reliable and an unreliable way of finding out the answers to these questions—and the reliable way is the way of scientific inquiry.

It is beginning to be clear that a good deal of the criticism of Dewey's theories of education is based fundamentally upon a rejection of the view that scientific psychology should be our guide to the problems of effective teaching. For obviously, if the results of modern education (granting that it, too, wants to teach the three Rs) are unsatisfactory as compared with the results of traditional education when dealing with matched children, nothing could be easier than to make the necessary changes in methods and tech-

niques, and no one would be more willing than modern
educators.

What is surprising, however, is that the very critics
who attack Dewey and modern education for their
alleged anti-intellectualism refuse to abide by the consequences of scientific inquiry into matters of disputed
fact. They do not even call for such inquiry. A very
instructive illustration of this is provided by the Council for Basic Education Inc., an educational pressure
group of growing influence, which is fanatically opposed to Dewey's educational philosophy and all practices based on it. It is the source of many of Admiral
Rickover's views on modern education. In one of its
official Bulletins (February 1958), it discusses "The
Seven Deadly Dogmas of Elementary Education," all
of which it derives from what it calls "the official
philosophy of education which has prevailed in the
past 30 years"—a euphemism for the complex of ideas
and theories associated with Dewey.

One of these seven deadly dogmas is listed as the
dogma of scientific knowledge. According to this
dogma, modern educators believe "that psychological
and sociological research has established enough 'truths'
about the nature of the child and the learning process
to provide infallible guides to methods and even content in the education of the very young." Of course
it is only in the minds of these "intellectualists," not in
the mind of any sensible educator, that psychological
findings provide "infallible" rather than reliable guides
to method. The discussion, however, seeks to dispute
two pieces of knowledge won by scientific educational
psychology as reported in *The Three R's Plus* (University of Minnesota, 1956). One is that "division by
two-place numbers is too difficult for fourth-graders
and should be postponed until the sixth"; the other is
"that children of average ability do not profit" from
the teaching of grammar. (Incidentally, the writer in

the Bulletin of the Council for Basic Education does not report the statements accurately. The first asserts that division by two-place numbers is too difficult for *average* fourth-graders; the second states that children of average ability do not profit from the teaching of grammar "of the old kind"—that is, formal instruction in parts of speech which have no reference to the expression of ideas. The inaccuracy of the reporting here—and not only here—is seriously misleading.)

The critical response of this exponent of classical and fundamental education to these claims of knowledge is not to challenge their truth on the basis of an examination of how they were reached, or by citation of other data won by controlled inquiry. He begins by denying "this glib faith in the ability of science and the scientific method to discover all truth about Man." But no one asserted that science can discover all the truth about Man. What has been asserted is a more modest proposition: Scientific inquiry shows that some methods of teaching some things are more effective than other methods. If this is to be denied, it is not enough to deny what no one asserts—*viz.,* that science can discover all the truth about anything. The more modest claim can be denied only on the basis of specific evidence.

The nearest the critic of modern education comes to providing such evidence is his report: "Fortunately there are still teachers whose own observation and common sense tell them most fourth-graders are not too underdeveloped to conquer the mysteries of division by two-place numbers and that English grammar properly taught is an immense aid to the competent and civilized use of one's own language." The fallacies of this criticism are apparent. No teacher can observe most fourth-graders. He or she can observe only the fourth-graders he or she knows. But this is a very small group; and unless there is reason to believe it is a

representative sample—that is, one not specially selected, something which requires scientific inquiry and
not merely common sense—it may be an extremely
unreliable index of most fourth-graders. Even if some
teachers make this report on the basis of a sample
about whose representative character we are not in
doubt, it would not tell us what most teachers observe.
It would, in any event, leave open the question as to
whose observations were more reliable. For it is not
merely the number of teachers who report observations
which counts, but the methods of observation and the
controls to which their observations have been subjected.

After all, we are concerned here with matters of
fact which are difficult but not impossible to determine
with a good degree of probability. Instead of exploring
this and similar questions, critics of modern education
wish to settle these matters by fiat, impressionism and
snap judgment. They do worse. They beg the question
because they fail to locate the problem. The question
is not whether "English grammar properly taught" is
helpful, but how it is "properly" taught—by instruction in formal parts of speech, diagramming, etc., or
by instruction through remedial analysis of mistakes
in usage and understanding.

What is even still worse than these elementary errors
in logic is the attempt to determine what are the facts
in the case by resort to political or ethical criteria.
"We believe," writes this critic, "that education
(which, after all, is supposed to change, remake and
refine the human animal) cannot be satisfied with some
norm of behavior, but must concern itself with what
ought to be." Even if it is true, in other words, that
most fourth-graders *cannot* learn some things, they
should learn them! But is it sensible to urge that one
should do what one can't do? Surely we must distinguish between situations where an "ought" implies

a "could" and situations where it is inapplicable. A child with normal hearing and vocal cords should learn to sing. But if he develops a bass voice, shall we insist that he "should" continue to sing alto or soprano? If we are dealing with a person who is tone deaf, "should" in this context is pointless.

The trouble with much of our education, John Dewey complained long before his critics, is that most children do not learn as much and as well as they can learn. Modern education, by enlisting scientific psychology, attempts to get them to learn as much and as well as they can. Its *program* is to hold the stick up to the very top level of each individual's capacity, and by engaging his interest, elicit the effort and drive that will take him as close to the top as possible. If it fails in this program, it is not because it is too scientific, but because it is not scientific enough. Of course, there are normative tasks which the school must face, and no one has stressed the importance of the moral aspects of education more than Dewey. But when it is relevant to ask the questions—What ought our behavior be? What is worth pursuing and possessing? What is the best thing to say or do in this situation?—can we improve on Dewey's reply that such questions are to be answered not by habit, not by drift, not by intuition, not by revelation, but by critical intelligence informed by all the relevant facts in the situation? And by intelligence he means the use of the *pattern* of scientific inquiry, as distinct from the specific techniques of specific subject matters. For Dewey, the ultimate authority in liberal civilization is the authority of scientific method, broadly interpreted as the method of intelligence.

This is not the place to analyze all of the alleged seven deadly dogmas of elementary education. They really are not dogmas but leading principles. And their discussion by the representatives of this pressure group betrays the one deadly sin of the life of the mind—the refusal to engage in inquiry in the face of a genuine problem. The real nub of the difference between Dewey and most of his critics of this and allied schools lies in the question of the nature of authority in human judgment. Whereas for Dewey authority is derived from the pattern of the self-corrective procedures of scientific method, for them this authority is subordinate to something else.

Every important thing Dewey said a half-century ago about education and society, and education and science (with the exception of some predictions about the future of vocational education), is even more valid today. He began to think about these questions when the world was rapidly changing. He argued that if education were conceived merely as the transmission of the culture of the past, youth would not really be prepared to meet and master the future. Today our world is changing at an even dizzier pace than he witnessed. The problems of mere survival, not to speak of survival and freedom, are greater than ever before. Nothing but intelligence *can* save us, but the chances that intelligence *will* are smaller than in the past.

Dewey's concept of intelligence involves the education of emotion, volition and perception, and not merely formal reasoning power or the exercise of what is sometimes called the *mind* or *intellect* considered in isolation from observation, experiment and practice. "There is no such thing as over-intellectuality," he wrote in *Democracy and Education*, "but there is such a thing as one-sided intellectuality."

If we reject scientific method, the method of free intelligence, as the supreme authority in judgment of both fact and value, what can we substitute in its stead? Every alternative involves at some point an institutional authority which, historical evidence shows, lends itself to abuse, which proclaims itself to be above all interests and becomes the expression of a particular interest invested with the symbols of public authority.

OBSTACLES AND OPPORTUNITIES

Dewey's educational philosophy must hurdle some great obstacles before it can be made socially effective. In a sense, this philosophy promises too much. As it conceives education, teaching becomes much more complex, much more of an art than conventional modes. It requires that teachers be much abler than most of them are at present likely to be: and it costs much more than most communities at present are willing to pay. It presupposes the existence of a humanist and scientific society in which all the large problems are being met in the spirit of Dewey's philosophy. The facts are otherwise and are likely to be so for a very long time. Where population is not controlled but grows by leaps and bounds, where practices of segregation and discrimination still exist, where an authoritarian parochial school system parallels the public school, where the presence and imminent threat of war engulfs the community so that the immediate necessities of national security must be given priority— a great deal of Dewey's educational philosophy appears to read like a counsel of perfection. It can do something, but to the literal-minded this will sometimes appear to be not very much.

In a crisis, no one seems to be concerned with the development of individual personalities as the basic categorical imperative of education. The public and even most educators are more concerned with *ad hoc* measures, which although justified are never sufficient. The very reaction against Dewey's philosophy of education is hard to explain in its own terms. If the

world were one democratic, freedom-loving, welfare
economy—which our own society cannot be so long
as its very existence is threatened by encroaching totalitarianism—Dewey's educational philosophy could very
well become widely accepted as *the* public educational
philosophy, although never an official ideology. But
that is a large "if," and there are many other "ifs."

This means that unless concerted political and social
efforts are made to strengthen the institutional framework of the democratic community, Dewey's educational philosophy may turn out to be inoperative. It
is not fortuitous that the Nazis would have none of it,
and that the Bolsheviks rejected all progressive educational practices as soon as they saw that Dewey's
philosophy was more interested in the personalities
of children than in their class antecedents. In a racialist
community it cannot be properly applied: nor in a
slum city which starves its schools, where municipal
administration is corrupt, where hoodlums and delin-
quents terrorize whole neighborhoods. Indeed, to
attempt to apply Dewey's educational philosophy
under manifestly unripe and hostile conditions may
result in consequences worse than those observable
in situations where conventional methods of discipline
and instruction prevail.

All this represents a two-fold challenge. First, it is
not enough to proclaim the virtues of the best system
of education for the best of all worlds. We must find
ways of making the best of this educational system in
a world which is far from the best. We must adapt,
modify, improvise in a creative way, using some features in one context and some in another, taking advantage of every opportunity to inch forward, like a New
York taxi driver—provided we know the direction
we are going. Each educator must work where he is,
with what he has, and strive to build up sympathetic
public opinion and public support on a local educa-

tional level. The intelligent teacher must make the loving parent his staunch auxiliary in this process.

Second, we must remember that we cannot succeed in education without succeeding in fields other than education—in community relations, in industry, in politics. Rates of progress are different in different fields and uncertain in all; but unless we can improve the quality of our local democratic communities, unless we can realize greater democracy in our personal lives and in our face-to-face relations with our neighbors, Dewey's educational philosophy will have only limited effectiveness.

In this sense, the battleground of education is co-terminous with the whole of society, for Dewey's educational philosophy entails and is entailed by his philosophy of liberalism. Intelligence in the service of freedom or free man must reconstruct social institutions so that they provide equal opportunity and equal concern for all. Only thus can we provide an educational philosophy not only for present-day America, but also for the future—a future in which, as Dewey envisaged it, "freedom and fullness of human companionship is the aim, and intelligent cooperative experimentation the method."

RELEVANT READING

Berkson, Isaac B., *The Ideal and the Community: A Philosophy of Education*. New York: Harper and Brothers, 1958.

Bestor, Arthur E., *Educational Wastelands*. Urbana: University of Illinois Press, 1953.

Bulletin of the Council for Basic Education, Washington, D.C., Vol. VII (March, 1963).

Dewey, John, *The Case of Leon Trotsky*. New York: Harper and Brothers, 1937.

——— "The Pragmatic Acquiescence." *New Republic* (January 25, 1927), p. 189.

Hocking, William E., *Experiment in Education*. New York: Regnery, 1954.

Hook, Sidney, *Education for Modern Man.* New York: Dial Press, Inc., 1946.

―――― "The Ends and Content of Education." *Daedalus,* LXXXVIII (Winter, 1959).

―――― *John Dewey: An Intellectual Portrait.* New York: The John Day Company, Inc., 1939.

――――, ed., *John Dewey: Philosopher of Science and Freedom. A Symposium.* New York: Dial Press, Inc., 1950.

Rickover, Hyman, *Education and Freedom.* New York: E. P. Dutton & Company, Inc., 1959.

The Philosophical Bases
of the Experience Curriculum

❀

Reginald D. Archambault

I. BASIC ASSUMPTIONS

The basic assumptions regarding knowledge, value, truth and being which serve as axioms for the experience curriculum movement are culled directly from the major tenets of pragmatism, with its strong reaction against the traditional dichotomy between theory and practice and truth and experience. The movement received its prime orientation from a new view of philosophy which emphasized human experience and its problems as the proper starting point for philosophic investigation. The emphasis in Darwin upon the life process as essentially a process of adjustment, and the Hegelian tendency toward the interrelation of apparent opposites into a single organic system—

This selection originally appeared in the the *Harvard Educational Review,* Summer, 1956.

these tendencies served as an impetus toward a new philosophic outlook based on adjustment, organicism and dynamism. John Dewey became the major exponent of the new movement, synthesizing the various emphases of other theorists: Peirce and the pragmatic view of truth; James and his emphasis on the interrelatedness of intellect and environment; and Mead with his emphasis on the social dynamics of human behavior. It remained for Dewey to develop these emphases into a coherent system utilizing the assumptions and insights of these men. The result is a tentative theory which employs a series of interrelated ideas stemming from the major axiom of experience as a process of life adjustment to a changing environment. Several corollaries follow from this axiom: the concept of knowledge as a process of reflective adjustment; the theory of learning as problem solving; the idea of the means-ends continuum and the organic relation between methods and objectives; the concept of needs, interests and habits as vital forces which give impetus to the process of life adjustment.

Since Dewey serves as the major spokesman for this group and interprets the main assumptions with an eye to their educational implications, we might consider these views, as presented by Dewey, in greater detail.

Theory of Knowledge

Since experience itself is a process of adjustment to a changing environment, knowledge is defined in terms of the interaction of the individual with a problematic situation which is bordered on the one hand by uncertainty, indecision and want, and on the other by a settled, resolved situation in which equilibrium has been re-established and the irritating factor has been removed through successful re-adjustment. Faced with a disturbing, problematic situation, the individual initiates the process of reflective thought. Dewey divides the process into five steps which should not be considered formal in any sense, but merely generally descriptive of the phases of thought as adjustment: (1) suggestions (leaping forward to a possible solution); (2) the isolation of the problem into a definite question; (3) the postulation of a tentative hypothesis; (4) the rehearsal in the imagination of various avenues of solution; (5) testing the hypothesis by overt or imaginative action.[1]

True learning, in the sense of intelligent, reflective behavior, takes place only when there is a purpose apparent to the learner. This purpose is an end-in-view, a possible solution to remove the felt need or lack, and to re-establish equilibrium. It follows that desire is an essential component of the learning process, for it establishes the impulse for adjustment which will be converted, through the learning process, into a definite habit, or mode of response. In retrospect, then, the process has three discernible characteristics: (1) observation; (2) knowledge of what has happened in similar situations in the past; and (3) judgment-reflection on what is observed.[2] As this cycle of reflective behavior is completed, and equilibrium is again restored, the organism readies itself to meet another problem of adjustment. Now he has an added store of personal experience to bring to bear upon new problems, a more complex and adaptive habit structure. The process is thus one of constantly "spiralling upward," a self-generating one which is nourished by experience to serve the future challenges of experience.

It is notable that Dewey uses this general schema

[1] John Dewey, *How We Think* (Boston: Heath, 1933), pp. 107 ff.

[2] John Dewey, *Experience and Education* (New York: Macmillan, 1938), p. 80.

as a framework of his theory of valuation as well. We will consider the latter in some detail in a later section.

The Nature of Ends

Among other dangerous and decadent dualisms inherited from traditional philosophy, the dichotomy between means and ends is for Dewey one of the most odious. Rather than an artificial separation between the two, Dewey points to their essential interrelatedness. He refers to the means-ends continuum, emphasizing the dynamic nature of the end-in-view which affects the character of the means chosen to attain it and the reciprocal component in the process—the necessity of the methods chosen to attain an end-in-view affecting the ultimate nature of the end itself. Ends-in-view are not final or fixed. They are rather tentative solutions which serve, in retrospect, as only a limited part of the totality of the consequences which result from a decided course of action. Thus the end which has been isolated in the imagination joins with other discernible results of the adjustment process to serve as a means toward a newly projected end-in-view, which in turn arises from a new problematic situation resulting from the flux of life adjustment.[3]

Ideal, fixed and immutable ends are inadmissible in this analysis because they are opposed to the dynamic interpretation of the process of learning as adjustment for continuous growth. The postulation of static ends is naive and dangerous. The admission of such ends is due to an inability to recognize the dynamic nature of the process of adjustment, the reciprocal relation between methods of attainment and projected solutions, and the connectedness of the totality of

[3] John Dewey, *Theory of Valuation* (Chicago: University of Chicago Press, 1939), p. 464.

consequences with the one aim which has been chosen as a directing focal point. The postulation of ideal ends which are incapable of human attainment is conducive to two undesirable alternatives. Either the individual, in searching for a real solution to practical problems, will become constantly frustrated and maladjusted because of the ineffectiveness of such a goal as a directing or stabilizing force; or the unreal end will persist as a vulgar symbol to which a lip-service is paid, but no commitment is actually given. Such artificial ends tend to arrest the process of growth by appealing to a previously existing and degenerate concept of truth and value, or misdirect growth by failing to set a true course for the adjustment process. Such ideal ends tend to negate the importance of experience itself and emphasize the mysterious and the supernatural, thus stultifying free inquiry into causes, consequences, and other natural relations.

In order to avoid such impediments to truth-seeking and understanding, and to encourage an enlightened improvement in human behavior, actions would be evaluated with reference to the consequences that they will entail, rather than with reference to external criteria. A careful and complete observation of the causal factors connected with an activity (the *means* to an end-in-view), and the totality of the discernible consequences of an activity, provide the proper method for objective evaluation.

The Nature of Goals and Objectives

It follows from the above analysis that goals must be discernible, tentative, subject to change with new desires and new environmental alterations. The concept of education as growth, and growth as the only admissible end for education follows directly from these principles. Growth must serve as its own end leading toward further, evolving growth, and education is the chief instrument for accelerating the growth process. Inherent in the concept of education as growth is the principle of continuity. Growth is not directionless, for it offers a fundamental directing criterion, insuring a healthy evolving life-adjustment process leading to further development and growth. Growth is a positive criterion then, for it insures future wholesome activity, and a perpetuation of the self-correcting life adjustment process.[4]

Inherent in these basic views, then, are the theoretical components of an educational theory which emphasized naturalism, scientific method and the dynamics of human experience. The problematic situation, the importance of the environment, the necessity of recognizing the needs and interests of the individual—all of these components serve as foundation points for a theory of education based on the experience of the learner.

II. APPLICATIONS TO EDUCATION

Problem Solving as a Basic Method

The direct theoretical application of Dewey's concept of knowledge as adjustment to problematic situations can best be exemplified with reference to William H. Kilpatrick's analysis of the optimum arrangement of the school situation for effective learning. It is notable that Kilpatrick follows Dewey's scheme directly by postulating five steps in the learning process: (1) A problematic situation which arises out of felt need of the child; (2) the analysis of the situation for the purpose of setting up tentative solu-

4 Dewey, *Experience and Education*, pp. 28 ff.

tions; (3) making plans and choosing from them; (4) testing the plan; (5) a backward look for an evaluation of the process. It is this scheme which serves as the basis for Kilpatrick's revolutionary project method which has had such a wide influence on school curricula and method.[5] Rugg and Shumaker in their highly influential volume *The Child-Centered School,*[6] and Caswell and Campbell in their basic text on Curriculum Development[7] are avid supporters of this general scheme. Paul R. Hanna presents this general scheme in a slightly more elaborate form, and William H. Burton uses it as a general description of learning and as a basis for a system of "directional process goals" which establish the framework of the entire school curriculum.[8] In the Thirty-Third Yearbook of the National Society for the Study of Education, which is devoted to an appraisal of the experience curriculum, there is a consensus on the validity of the principle itself and its concomitant idea of injecting life-imitating situations into the curriculum.[9] The principle of problem solving has been accepted as an ideal model for stimulating thought, arriving at results and adjustments which will be meaningful and satisfying to the students, and caring for individual differences in need and interests. The use of the unit plan as a basis for curriculum design serves to eliminate the danger of non-transference of school learning to life experiences by initiating life-imitative experiences within the school

[5] William H. Kilpatrick, *Remaking the Curriculum* (New York: Newson, 1936).

[6] Harold Rugg and Ann Shumaker, *The Child-Centered School* (Chicago: World Book, 1928).

[7] Hollis L. Caswell and Doak S. Campbell, *Curriculum Development* (New York: American Book, 1935). See especially Chapter VIII.

[8] See William H. Burton, *The Guidance of Learning Activities* (New York: Appleton-Century-Crofts, Inc., 1952), pp. 328–329.

[9] National Society for the Study of Education, *XXXIII Yearbook,* 1934.

curriculum itself. William H. Burton offers an analysis of the development of the scheme, emphasizing its directing force:

1. Problems arise out of the felt needs of the student.
2. These needs are related, in the process of the unit, to wider areas of experience. This is achieved through cooperative teacher-pupil planning.
3. In the process of developing the unit, skills are incorporated as needed by the student in order to solve a specific problem which is meaningful for him as an individual and for the group as a whole.
4. The completion of such a task furnishes further experience which can subsequently be used in building more units of increasing difficulty.
5. As the child grows, and his experience accumulates and broadens, his interests, needs and wants grow to be similar to those of the adult society.[10]

This is a reaction against the formalized prescription of a static subject matter from without, which might tend to stultify and misdirect the genuine needs and interests of the students, and to impose external goals which are either beyond or in conflict with the goals of the students. The educative process becomes an evolving one, determining subject matter content from within by cooperative pupil-teacher planning.

The Role of Interest and Needs in Curriculum Design

The common problem of the divergence between interest and discipline disappears in the experience curriculum, because the felt needs and immediate interests of the learner serve as the impetus for the learning process. Cooperative teacher-pupil planning insures a curricular project which will satisfy the desires of the student and makes the interest factor the essential component which initiates the selection

[10] Burton, *op. cit.,* Chapter 4.

of the setting for learning and the material to be studied. Since the task is meaningful and purposeful, interest is not introduced as a mere frill or sugar-coating in order to make a task more palatable; it is rather an essential component of the learning process itself.

The term "need" is often used interchangeably with that of "interest." Dewey, however, is careful to distinguish among need, interest and purpose. Need is defined as an irritation or lack which initiates the quest for adjustment. Purpose is defined as a *sustained* desire—one which is proven to be more than fleeting and momentary. Interest is described as a bond which unites the material to be studied with the effort of the learner. Interest is therefore an essential catalyst in the learning process, but one which is always present as a by-product of genuine purpose operating to insure the absorption of the child in a learning task which is both challenging and meaningful for him. Therefore, learning arises out of a felt need which sustains itself sufficiently to become a compelling purpose. Interest arises automatically and naturally sustains itself as the solution to the problematic situation offers a challenging and magnetic attraction for the learner.

It might be noted that the need for imposed discipline disappears. Dewey notes that the true definition of discipline is best understood as the ability of an individual to see a task through to its conclusion. Although admitting that imposed discipline might sometimes be essential in the school as it is in life, he insists that a learning situation which stems from real problems to which a student can be committed, would eliminate an extensive need for imposed discipline. The need for imposed discipline in the traditional setting for learning arises not from the innate mischievous nature of the child, but from the dull and routine tasks to which he is assigned. These tasks do not call for work, but drudgery, for they force the child to sustain himself in an activity which is divorced from any genuine meaning and interest for his every day life problems. A curriculum which sought its rationale and orientation in the life experiences of the learner, rather than in a body of abstract thought essentially divorced from life, would insure maximum commitment to the task at hand and eliminate the chief source of the need for imposed discipline.[11]

Most adherents of the doctrine of interest recognize the severe limitations of the unqualified concept of interest alone as a criterion for creating a setting for learning. Kilpatrick, while affirming the importance of the doctrine of interest as an initiating factor in the learning process, points to the need for the development of this original felt need into a sustained interest or purpose which will serve as a unifying force in the learning situation.[12] Caswell and Campbell, defining interest as "the attitude developed through a pleasant or satisfying experience," emphasize both the importance and the limitations of the concept.[13] They consider interest to be important chiefly because of its fundamental relation to pupil purpose. Interests are defined as representing deep-lying attitudes rather than passing whims or fancies, and these in turn should be projected into long range purposes.

The important point to be made here is that the more sophisticated advocates of the experience curriculum are not satisfied with immediate interests, impulses, or desires as the basis of curriculum design. The doctrine of interest is modified by reference to "persistent" and "sustained" interests, but the criterion for differentiation between mere "passing fancies" and

[11] John Dewey, *Democracy and Education* (New York: Macmillan, 1916), pp. 146–161.
[12] Kilpatrick, *op. cit.,* p. 25.
[13] Caswell and Campbell, *op. cit.,* pp. 209 ff.

more significant and worthy interests is often lacking. If we look to Dewey, however, we note that he attempts to clarify the issue by appealing to his description of intelligent behavior, and this same rationale seems to be implicit in other works which stem from the same basic theory of knowledge. For Dewey, the democratic process of social intelligence—pupil-teacher give and take—can lead to a criterion for the meaningfulness and importance of a specific activity, and the subsequent direction which it can pursue. This does not necessitate the imposition of direction by the teacher. The process should be one in which the teacher is a guiding factor, to accept and develop pupil suggestions, and to help the students organize them into a meaningful whole. The emphasis here is upon the intellect, the ability of social intelligence to arrive at progressive decisions which will distinguish the meaningless and superficial from the meaningful and significant. Thus the conclusion is sought within a consistent framework of experience, for there is no reference to an ulterior standard or value.[14] The emphasis rests upon the importance of the unique situation and the totality of the consequences of an individual decision in its effect upon the social group. An intelligent analysis of the dynamics of the unique learning situation through careful teacher guidance, then, will suffice in furthering the growth process, satisfying individual needs, and developing fruitful and rewarding experiences for the individual and the group as a whole.

The role of the teacher in this scheme becomes quite apparent. He is not merely a negative factor in the learning process, for his prime function is to interpret the needs and interests of the group, and to help to guide these into potentially rewarding channels of activity—"to see that the occasion is taken

[14] Dewey, *Experience and Education,* Chapter VI.

advantage of." Due to his wealth of previous experience and his superior fund of knowledge, the guidance given by the teacher in his role of leader in the cooperative enterprise is an aid to pupil freedom, rather than a restriction upon it. He aids the students to seize upon purposes which they cannot objectify without guidance. The endeavor is cooperative and not dictatorial, investigative rather than prescriptive. Thus the role of the teacher becomes most important because he must survey the previous experiences and interests of his students, and analyze the current and unique school situation in all of its facets in order to help manifest the potential for growth and adjustment in all of his students. The prescription of a static subject matter scheme would only stultify this opportunity for creative guidance on the part of the teacher, and tend to mold the students into a stultifying and prescribed framework.[15]

It follows, therefore, that the curriculum must not be based upon a prescribed subject matter which is imposed from above. Such a view fails to take into account the nature of the learner, the dynamic process of learning and thinking, and the necessarily tentative nature of goals and objectives. John Brubacher states:

On the whole, this theory (the traditional subject-matter approach) tends to the dualistic. It sets the child on one hand over against the whole paraphernalia of instruction on the other. The aims of education . . . are set forth for the child by the teacher, his parents, and the adult community. The curriculum, too, represents adult interests and is set before him in the form of subject matter to be learned. The order of the lesson, that is, the order of presentation of the subject matter, is organized logically to conform to the external and ingrained order of the universe itself.[16]

[15] *Ibid.,* Chapter VI.
[16] John S. Brubacher, *Modern Philosophies of Education* (New York: McGraw, 1950), p. 254.

Burton sums up the general attitude of this group towards a curriculum composed of a static and pre-scribed subject matter:

The logical arrangement of the subject matter is that of the adult, of the informed person, of the mature mind. It is for the sake of the subject matter itself. Such organiza-tion fractionizes the world for the immature learner. The child lives in a concrete personal world in which his prac-tical purposes, desires, and emotional reactions are the threads of organization. He is not and should not be con-cerned with subject matter as such. He uses material from any and all sources as he needs to solve a problem and satisfy some desire. Hence, he attacks and masters subject matter not as it is logically and systematically organized but as it happens to fit his pursuits and purposes.[17]

III. CONTROVERSIAL ISSUES

The Ambiguity of the Concept of Interest

The prime difficulty involved in the postulation of pupil interest as a criterion of curriculum content lies in the failure of its proponents to present a convincing proof that the doctrine is both necessary and sufficient. The main attack of the new group on the traditionalist camp rests on the attempt to show that the older views erred in failing to take account of interest as a *necessary* consideration in curriculum planning. The views of Brubacher and Burton are directly applicable here. However, it should be noted that the burden of proof regarding the *sufficiency* of the doctrine of interest as a basis for planning, rests upon the adherents of the new and radical view. We have noted some of the attempts to modify the doctrine in order to accom-modate a further criterion for determining the selection of the interests which are to be nurtured and guided

[17] Burton, *op. cit.*, p. 407.

into more persistent patterns of behavior. Perhaps it would be fruitful to analyze these major attempts with an eye to their completeness.

The argument from purpose serves to point to the need for further qualification of the interest criterion, and in itself begs the question by failing to establish it. It is one thing to maintain that the more significant and potentially beneficial interests are those which should be seized upon and encouraged; it is quite another thing to point to the *standard* for discovering those interests. Dewey introduces a further qualification by appealing to the method of group intelligence and the need for recognizing the needs of the group, examining the possible consequences of a chosen activity, and bringing previous experience to bear upon the problem of selection. The emphasis here is upon the uniqueness of the particular learning situation, and the danger of applying hard and fast rules of selection. However, these considerations fail to clarify the problem of a standard of selection for a teacher faced with a multiplicity of various possible directions and a privilege to proceed *carte blanche*. Those activities which are nurtured and developed into persistent patterns will affect the future behavior patterns, values, and interests of the child. We have noted that the teacher's role is not a merely negative one here. But the role of the teacher as interpreted by Dewey is strangely paradoxical. It is certainly not clear whether the teacher is in fact directing the learning process or whether he acts merely as a neutral catalyst in the process. Dewey seems to be in the common position of wanting to eat his cake and have it as well. If the teacher is in fact imposing direction from above, then one might be justified in asking just what is the rationale for the choice—a justification which rests on something more than mere expediency. If, on the other hand, the teacher is merely a neutral factor who organizes the environment in such a way as to allow for the full development of the child's natural interests, then a strong argument might be made against this tacit assumption of a static potential inherent in the learner. Dewey has certainly rejected this view in his invectives against Rousseau. The postulation of a middle course which calls for a cooperative effort at pupil-teacher planning serves only to cloud the issue by dispersing the responsibility for choice among a larger group, but fails to come to grips with the real underlying issue—the standard for judgment.

There is another major line of defense for justifying the use of pupil interest and need as basic to content selection. Both Kilpatrick and Burton point to the role of objectives as "directional process goals" or "emerging and evolving objectives." For Kilpatrick, goals emerge from individual purposes which become more clearly defined as they manifest themselves more fully. Thus, specialization, interest in subject matter, and an awareness of wider social values automatically emerge out of the growth process as the child's fund of experience grows as a result of the educative process.[18] But here the role of individual immediate interest is emphasized more than in the Dewey analysis. The tacit assumption here is that the unburdened intellect of the child will assure an automatic development which will not only be valuable and beneficial, but which will incidentally culminate in an acceptance of and commitment to, societal values. Yet there seems to be no indication that this guarantee is valid, even if it is admitted that "societal values" should be cherished. If we admit the importance of the environment in shaping the habits, character, and values of the individual, this would seem to indicate the strong probability that specific values would not receive

[18] Kilpatrick, *op. cit.*, pp. 105 ff., 113 ff.

assent unless the environment for learning provided for a pattern of experiences which would in fact be directed toward this aim.

In Burton's postulation of "directional process goals" there is an attempt to synthesize the major tenets of all of the above views. The teacher is to recognize and nurture the immediate interests of the learner in order to provide a stimulating and meaningful setting for learning. These interests are in turn directed toward the teacher's goals—the acquisition of skills, the development of an interest in a particular area of study. The teacher is in turn expected to relate these activities to the broader needs and goals of society. Therefore, the scheme attempts to accommodate the needs and interests of the student by utilizing them as a starting point for learning, while at the same time calling for accepted cultural values to serve as the ultimate justification for curriculum content.

The difficulty in this scheme would seem to rest on the question as to whether such a scheme would not in fact be in great danger of sabotaging its own objectives. If societal values are the ultimate goal of instruction, together with a subsidiary but related goal of subject matter proficiency, one might well question whether this scheme would not in fact lead to an essentially haphazard organization, an uncertainty of direction and purpose, and a general indecisiveness regarding the relative importance of immediate interests and broader objectives. If the major aim is really the achievement of broader needs, then the use of fleeting interests as a basis of organization would at best lead to a highly uneconomical pattern of procedure. Furthermore, since the importance of the broader values is logically prior to the individual needs, it would seem much more realistic to postulate these goals and their correlative skills and attitudes as basic ends rather than peripheral considerations which will be allowed in the back door as they may become useful in solving personally meaningful problems. This seems to be a particularly confusing juxtaposition of means and ends to the extent that their logical and causal interpretations are not only divorced but are also in opposition to one another.

The ambiguities and difficulties inherent in the concept of interest and its relation to learning and curriculum has become more apparent as time has gone on. Faced with the danger of deteriorating value structure in the 1930's, the experimentalists began searching for a new emphasis regarding the nature of educational ends. The shift in emphasis was most apparent in Dewey himself:

There is nothing in the bare concept of activity that gives helpful direction to the educational program. There must be the kind and amount of doing that conduces to health and vigor, that produces observation and reflection, that clarifies and tests ideas, that tempers while it expresses emotions. No set program can be deduced from these generalities. They define a problem to be met by continued observation and experimentation, the solutions never being twice alike with different individuals or different groups. The settled point is that activity as doing is a means rather than an end. . . . The problem is to discover within present experience those values that are akin to those which the community prizes, and to cultivate those tendencies that lead in the direction that social demands will take.[19]

Growth, Values and Objectives

The tendency to insist upon experience alone supplying its own ends, while denying the validity of the admission of external goals, clearly serves as the source of the difficulty in the experimentalist view in general, and in the thought of Dewey in particular. The in-

[19] John Dewey, National Society for the Study of Education, *XXXIII Yearbook,* pp. 83–84.

adequacy of this approach can best be exemplified by pointing to the supposedly complete and self-justifying concept of growth as an educational end. In spite of attempted defenses of the view by Dewey and his followers emphasizing the inadequacy of distorted criticisms of the view, we seem to be left with little in the way of a tangible criterion which could direct the educative process. Dewey points out quite justifiably that the true meaning of growth implies a dynamic process of positive and healthy development. Hence the criticisms which point to "destructive growth" and "malignant growth" fail to recognize the essential meaning of the concept. This can be admitted. But this is merely a precondition for any healthy activity—that it must not be self-defeating. It points to the necessity for an examination of long-run consequences as well as the need for an observation of the merely immediate effects of a course of action. In essence, however, insistence upon education to further growth is a negative concept in that it merely calls for the abandonment of imposed goals which might deter the growth process. We can all admit that nothing must be allowed to interfere with healthy development, but we are still left with the need for establishing a standard for ascertaining exactly what *is* healthy in a given instance. Implicit in this belief in the inherent goodness of growth is the idea that free development will automatically lead to progress through the strengthening of the modes of intelligent adaptation, a broader and less self-centered orientation toward problems, and improvement through understanding.

It is at this point that we see most clearly the interrelatedness of educational theory and its fundamental problems, with the ethical foundation on which it is based. The attempt at the establishment of a scientific ethic self-consciously divorced from traditional values, and the refusal to admit "external" criteria for moral judgment has its parallel in the refusal to admit the inclusion of established values as a stabilizing and directing factor in educational planning. In the final analysis it becomes apparent that a broad view of the causes and consequences related to a unique activity is not in itself sufficient for establishing a basis of commitment for ethics. Dewey himself seems to recognize the inadequacy of his original experimental approach when he points to the need for the recognition of persistent societal values in order to establish a firmer foundation for judgment, and a basis for direction in the postulation of educational ends. Rather than a mere shift in emphasis, however, this modification seems to indicate a rejection of mere experimentalism in the search for ends. If we accept the assumption that persistent societal values are to be used as ultimate bases of commitment, then this throws the entire process of valuing and end-making into a significantly new perspective.

The tendency of Dewey and others to emphasize the dynamic interrelation between means and ends in a practical context serves to eliminate the static dualism between the two which has haunted philosophy. Yet the emphasis on this practical relation in a live context tends to obscure the logical distinction between means and ends which can and must be differentiated. To say that the two cannot be divorced is only half true, for they must be divorced in imagination if we are to understand the true meaning of the concepts. Ends represent aims, focal points for action —desirable goals which are deserving of attainment and worthy of pursuit. These ends need not receive their justification from a supernatural or unreal source, but they must be justified on a more permanent, consistent, and inclusive base than mere desire in an immediate situation. It is possible to work within the realm of human experience with its accumulation of knowledge to discover values which are persistent and meaningful for a variety of contexts, and which can serve as the core for a value system. These initial commitments need not be ideal or fixed and could be conducive to change and adjustment to new ethical situations. But the essential point here is that these values would stand outside the limited context of naturalistic factors involved in choice, and serve as standards of judgment for the process itself.

Dewey, in his later writings, seems aware of the need for such a standard to serve as a directing force for the educative process. If the need for such criteria is admitted, then the recognition of the need for the logical distinction between means and ends would be particularly relevant. With a clear idea of educational goals based on these criteria, the way would be clear for the establishment of a curriculum which would be most conducive to the promotion of these goals. Methods could then be evaluated with an eye to their effectiveness in fulfilling their established function. There would be more attention to economy, and to the appraisal of tangible educative results.

This distinction does not necessitate a set of formal, traditional, ideal or static goals which are arbitrarily imposed and true for all time. It does, however, allow for the inclusion of a stabilizing force for establishing a direction and form for education.

CONCLUSION

It seems apparent that the limitations of the philosophic bases of the experience curriculum are significant. Aside from the ambiguities in the concepts basic to the view, the prime difficulty lies in the severe limitations placed upon ends, aims and values. The scheme is faulty primarily because of its insistence upon the exclusion of concepts which are not directly related to the context of adjustment in a unique situation. As a result, the scheme is basically inadequate. These inadequacies have led to widespread excesses in learning-by-doing, activity for its own sake, and the abuses connected with free and uninhibited activity. Certainly all of these abuses cannot be directly attributed to the experimentalist scheme. Yet it is also true that the scheme did not contain within itself the necessary discipline and thoroughness which would avoid such widespread abuses and misinterpretations. The traditional subject-matter orientation toward curriculum has long suffered from an inability to recognize the importance of child interest, problem solving, and sound methodology. It has tended to set up goals which were essentially divorced from a consideration of the nature of the learner. In this sense there is much value which can be derived from the emphasis of the experimentalists. Here is where the great value of the movement lies. The traditional view has its strongest advantage in its recognition of the need for establishing sound goals for education. The recent tendency to expand the base of the experience movement to admit more tangible and persistent aims and values seems to pose a fruitful area for the potential synthesis of the two broad views. The result of such a synthesis would be an educational theory which would capitalize on the advances in methodology which the experimentalists have nurtured and perfected, while using these methods as means toward a tangible but tentative set of goals. Let us hope that the recognition of the necessity for such a synthesis will be soon forthcoming.

RELEVANT READING

Archambault, R. D., "The Concept of Need in its Relation to Certain Aspects of Educational Theory." *Harvard Edu-*

cational Review, XXVII (Winter, 1957).

———— ed., *John Dewey on Education*. New York: The Modern Library, 1964.

———— ed., *John Dewey's Lectures in Philosophy of Education: 1899*. New York: Random House, Inc., 1966.

Bode, Boyd H., *Progressive Education at the Crossroads*. New York: Newson & Company, 1938.

Dewey, John, "Interest as Related to the Training of the Will." *Second Supplement to the Herbart Year Book for 1895*. Bloomington, Ill., 1896.

Ulich, Robert, *History of Educational Thought*. New York: American Book Company, 1945, pp. 315–336.

Progressive Education

———————————————

John Dewey and Progressive Education Today

❀

M. I. Berger

It is ironical that John Dewey remains today at the center of a conflict in American education. The man who dedicated himself to the task of reconciling apparently antithetical positions in education provoked a new era of conflict. There are several reasons why Dewey became and has remained a controversial figure in education. First, the obscurity of some of his writing led many to misunderstand him. Second, there were many who, sincerely believing they were following the ideas of Dewey, brought forth new conceptions that contradicted or went far away from Dewey's own belief. (In part, Dewey is to blame for this development, since he left many questions unanswered. Indeed, his educational writings left the explicit consequences of his ideas for others to devise.) Nevertheless, these ideas, although they often did not agree with the philosopher's notions, were identified with his conception of education. Finally, there are many who have attacked Dewey but never have troubled themselves to read and examine his meanings.

What was Dewey's educational position? The most common fallacy is that Dewey is the father of Progressive education and, consequently, is responsible for all that emerged from this movement. Actually, Pro-

This selection appeared originally in *School and Society,* March, 1959. Professor Berger teaches at Albany State College.

gressive education was, in great measure, independent
of Dewey's ideas. Many would be startled to know
that Dewey devoted a large part of his efforts to
criticizing the basic assumptions of Progressive educators. One of the most important contributions of
the American philosopher was that he tried to reconcile
the split between Progressivists and Traditionalists by
showing that both philosophies were vital and proper
in the scheme of education. There are two works of
the man that clearly show him trying to reconcile these
differences: "The Child and the Curriculum" (1902)
and "Experience and Education" (1938).

Which is more important in education, the child or
the curriculum? Progressivists would say the child
with all his needs and interests should be respected
above all else; personality and character, freedom and
initiative, spontaneity, and change—these are the
keynotes of the Progressive theme. Traditionalists, on
the other hand, emphasize the curriculum, the heritage
of the past, the funded experiences of mankind; knowledge and information, guidance and discipline, the old
and the past—these values stream forth from the traditionalist camp. Who is right? Dewey, in "The Child
and the Curriculum," says both schools of thought,
in their proper places, are correct:

Abandon the notion of subject matter as something fixed
and ready-made in itself, outside the child's experience;
cease thinking of the child's experience as also something
hard and fast; see it as something fluent, embryonic, vital;
and we realize that the child and the curriculum are simply
two limits which define a single process. Just as two points
define a straight line, so the present standpoint of the child
and the facts and truths of studies define instruction. It
is continuous reconstruction moving from the child's
present experience out into that represented by the organized bodies of truth we call studies (p. 11).

For Dewey, then, both the child and the curriculum are important in the educative process. The problem is not that of choosing one or the other but devising a way to bring the child with all his experiences to understand and assimilate the wealth of our culture. He continues,

. . . The radical fallacy . . . is that we have no choice save either to leave the child to his own unguided spontaneity or to inspire direction upon him from without. Action is response; it is adaptation, adjustment. There is no such thing as sheer self activity possible—because all activity takes place in a medium, in a situation, and with reference to its conditions. But, again, no such thing as imposition of truth from without, as insertion of truth from within, is possible. All depends upon the activity which the mind itself undergoes in responding to what is presented from without. Now the value of the formulated wealth of knowledge that makes up the course of study is that it may enable the educator *to determine the environment of the child,* and thus by indirection to direct. Its primary value, its primary indication, is for the teacher, not the child. It says to the teacher: Such and such are the capacities, the fulfillments, in truth and beauty and behavior, open to these children. Now see to it that day by day the conditions are such that *their own activities* move inevitably in this direction, toward such culmination of themselves. Let the child's nature fulfil its own destiny, revealed to you in whatever of science and art and industry the world now holds as its own (pp. 30–31).

Dewey was trying to move away from the formulation of educational problems in terms of an Either-Or philosophy. As stated, traditional and Progressive education, in their proper context, are appropriate. Just as surely, both philosophies, when falsely stressed, are wrong. Traditional education, when it emphasized the curriculum without regard for the learner, made a mistake. Progressive education, when it devoted all its energies to the child and ignored all external authority, when it ignored the importance of subject matter, was equally wrong. As Dewey states in "Experience and Education,"

. . . When external authority is rejected, the problem becomes that of finding the factors of control that are inherent within experience. When external authority is rejected, it does not follow that all authority should be rejected, but rather that there is need to search for a more effective source of authority. Because the older education imposed the knowledge, methods, and rules of conduct of the mature person upon the young, it does not follow, except on the basis of the extreme Either-Or philosophy, that the knowledge and skill of the mature person have no directive value for the experience of the immature. On the contrary, basing education upon personal experience may mean more multiplied and more intimate contacts between the mature and the immature than ever existed in the traditional school, and consequently more, rather than less, guidance by others . . . (p. 8).

Above all else, Dewey continues, it is wrong to attach allegiance to one philosophy or another simply because of its name. Neither Progressive education nor traditional education is unquestionably good. The only worth-while cause is that of improving education.

I have used frequently . . . the words "progressive" and "new" education. I do not wish to close, however, without recording my firm belief that the fundamental issue is not of new versus old education nor of progressive against traditional education but a question of what anything whatever must be to be worthy of the name *education*. I am not, I hope and believe, in favor of any ends or any methods simply because the name progressive may be applied to them. The basic question concerns the nature of education with no qualifying adjectives prefixed. What we want and need is education pure and simple, and shall make surer and faster progress when we devote ourselves to finding out just what education is and what conditions

have to be satisfied in order that education may be a
reality and not a name or a slogan . . . (pp. 115–116).

It appears that parents and educators have approached Dewey and his philosophy in three different
ways. Some have stopped before reaching Dewey,
assuming without examination that the man is "bad"
and should not be read, let alone followed. Others
have gone right past Dewey never stopping to examine
his ideas; they have emerged with what they believe is
truly "progressive" education, although actually their
ideas are in no way related to Dewey. Not too many
have gone through Dewey's writings, examining his
ideas in light of present conditions, judging their
worth, and reconstructing new programs in teaching
that in part accept and in part modify Dewey's conceptions.

Any hope for the intelligent improvement of educational practice seems to rest with the third approach.
Much of what Dewey advocated has not been realized.
In large part, our schools have been pouring new wines
into old bottles. Only snatches of Dewey's ideas have
crept into the schools. Nor are the schools entirely at
fault. Dewey's educational program is a fantastically
difficult one to realize—certainly it cannot come about
in one or even two generations. The philosopher's
plan involved far more than simply installing moveable
furniture or having people sit in circles. In his scheme
of things, an entire climate emerges—a democratic
climate. We lose sight of the purpose of our schools
when we think that our only mission is to teach people
more and more factual knowledge in the best possible
way. Fascist and communist societies also teach facts
—and very effectively. What we must also remember
is that we are trying to educate people for a way of life
and in a manner that reflects this way of life. Facts
alone will never make men free. Nor can a society that

creates an exclusive elite of the intelligent claim to be
democratic. Here is the soul of Dewey's entire
philosophy: a system of education that best recognizes
the dignity and worth of all individuals, that allows
every individual to develop to his fullest, and that
teaches the virtues of democracy by establishing a
democratic atmosphere.

Finally, Dewey needs to be corrected and modified.
If Dewey were to be resurrected, he undoubtedly
would be the first man to criticize his own ideas. His
metaphysical foundation, the idea that we live in a
dynamic world where conditions and ideas change,
would compel him to do so. Dewey, at the turn of the
century, could not foresee an atomic age, which, with
all its promised goodness, also has accentuated the anxiety of young people about tomorrow. Dewey did not
make explicit the differences in the different levels of
learning. Children learn as children, but adolescents
have different interests and different problems, and
similarly, adults cannot be taught the same way we
teach children. There cannot be one method that will
resolve the problems of "education." Each level needs
to work out its own way of teaching. Equally important, each school needs to understand the uniqueness of
its students and create a proper educational program
for *that* school and in *that* time.

Dewey remains a seminal figure in the history of
modern educational thought. He brought forth new
ways to solve old problems. He, more than any other
man, brought democracy and education to a systematic
unity. He remains a great thinker to be read, understood, and modified.

RELEVANT READING

Bode, Boyd H., *Progressive Education at the Crossroads*. New
    York: Newson & Company, 1938.

Dewey, John, *My Pedagogic Creed*. New York: E. L. Kellogg
    and Company, 1897.
—— *Progressive Education and the Science of Education*.
    Washington: Progressive Education Association, 1928.
—— "Comment." *The Activity Movement*, Yearbook XXXIII,
    Part II, National Society for the Study of Education.
    Bloomington: Public School Publishing Company, 1934.
Handlin, Oscar, "Rejoinder to Critics of John Dewey." *New
    York Times Magazine* (June 15, 1958).

Who Wants Progressive Education?

THE INFLUENCE OF JOHN DEWEY
ON THE PUBLIC SCHOOLS

❧

Albert Lynd

European domination of American educational theory
ended with the nineteenth century. Professor John
Dewey, long of Columbia University but then of the
University of Chicago, published *The School and
Society* in 1899. For most of the last half-century the
"philosopher of science and freedom" who died in
1952 was the strongest influence upon the New Education in America.

In the history of educational reform, the transition
from the romanticism of Rousseau and Pestalozzi to
the scientific pragmatism of Dewey is remarkable. More
remarkable is the association of Dewey's name with
the current literature of the New Education. Much

This selection appeared originally in *The Atlantic Monthly,* April,
1953 (Copyright 1953, by Albert Lynd). Mr. Lynd is a layman with
a long-standing interest in the schools.

of it consists of insipid incantations about growth and richness and joy and the rest of the jargon which passes for bold new thinking in neo-pedagogy; a jargon which one professor of philosophy described as a series of "emotive, question-begging words and phrases."

There is a probable explanation. Much of the writing and speaking on behalf of the New Education is done by persons who understand what is easy to understand, that Mr. Dewey has given them license to chop down something: the traditional curriculum and discipline. Chopping is an occupation many find agreeable; they are less clear about what they should do to replace what they are destroying. Their efforts to make this intelligible in the books and articles which they write for one another may be responsible for most of the inanities of neo-pedagogy.

When some notorious reactionary-by-trade denounces the fundamental pragmatism of Dewey as subversive of traditional religion and of economic liberalism (which it is) the Neo-Educationists rush into print to denounce the pamphleteer's grubby motives. But a frank defense of pragmatism with a clear statement to the public of what it really implies is not usually included. The writings of Dewey himself and of his disciples (Kilpatrick, Rugg, Bode, and others), in which these statements are to be found, are by their nature not likely to fall in the way of many plain parents and citizens. It is left to pamphleteering bagmen to explain Dewey to a public consisting largely of parents who have an anxious stake in educational theory.

I respect Dewey's genius and his rugged intellectual integrity. His prose is not fluent, but it has a powerful effect even upon a layman without philosophical pretensions. No matter how far you are from agreement with him, you must admire his systematic pommeling of every trace of what he finds amiss in time-honored systems of ideas. If some of those happen to be ideas which you believe to be important, the experience is like watching someone bludgeon your grandmother while proving to you that she clearly deserves it.

The catch is that there are other eminent philosophers who will expertly rehabilitate your grandmother. The most important question here is not whether Dewey's views of the nature of man and the universe are right or wrong. That is as you please. But Mr. Dewey's importance is not lessened by asking: How many parents would agree that his ideas, if they understood them, are those which should determine the formation of their children? And how many communities, if consulted, would be likely to approve a philosophy which is plainly uncongenial to certain loyalties which most plain nonphilosophizing people hold, for better or worse, to be important: belief in supernaturalism, in a transcendent natural law, in the immutability of certain moral principles?

In my experience with such discussions, this is the point at which a New Educationist may forget his theoretical devotion to democracy: he may rush in with the statement that "ordinary people" are not competent judges of philosophical or educational theory. That may be true, but it begs the next question: If we must have one dominant philosophical influence upon the reform of our schools, who voted for Dewey? There are many competing philosophies which enjoy intellectual (and democratic) respectability today. How did one philosophy acquire in lower education a dominance quite out of proportion to its standing—considerable as it is—among professional philosophers? And fantastically out of proportion to popular agreement with its basic principles?

Dewey's great influence upon American education is usually explained by his disciples on the ground that his philosophy is peculiarly congenial to the spirit of

American democracy. That is not wholly convincing: the argument is circular, because it includes conceptions of democracy which are themselves a part of Mr. Dewey's philosophy. His authority is more probably explainable as an historical accident; he was the only first-rate American philosopher to take an intense, evangelical interest in the lower schools. For our graduates in Education who are uneducated in anything but their own trade, Dewey is to the American school what Aristotle was to the medieval school: simply "the Philosopher." His name is used as a charm within the profession and an exorcism without. This is an interesting fate for the century's most consistent foe of dogmatism.

II

Dewey's educational theories are consistently related to his basic philosophical views. What are those views? We have a problem here. Any attempt to reduce to capsule explanations a complex set of ideas will certainly irritate its professional expounders, and with some reason, because oversimplification entails the risk of misrepresentation. But it should be even more irritating to a parent to be told that without technical philosophical training he cannot expect to understand the ideas which may be influencing the formation of his children. The following is simply a layman's distillation of Mr. Dewey's key ideas from those of his works which come nearest to general circulation. For my inadequacy here I apologize only to Mr. Dewey and to any Neo-Educationist who has made an effort to present a more competent *popular* exposition of the philosophy which determines his educational views.

Mr. Dewey's philosophy is usually called *instrumentalism.*

The implication is that knowledge is not merely the descriptive information acquired by the viewer of a scene; rather it is something which is begotten and exercised in action and which is an instrument for more intelligent action. Instrumentalism is a development of the *pragmatism* of William James. The essential principle of pragmatism is that the test of truth in a proposition is not in its source, but in "how it works." The following points are prominent in Dewey's thought:—

There are no eternal truths. From the beginning of intellectual history, men have argued about the truth or falsity of countless propositions, but they were usually agreed that there is such a thing as absolute truth. For Dewey, as for James, striving for immutable truth is futile. Dewey goes beyond James in elaborating the pragmatic principle through every area of philosophical concern, in relating it to modern experimental science, and in applying it to social problems.

The Deweyan theory of knowledge turns on an insistence that the old Greek dualism of mind and body is false. Man is wholly a biological organism. The mind does not learn or know as a spectator; rather, knowledge results from the interaction of the human organism with the environment. In this "continuum of experience" a human being is inextricably involved with other persons and things; the act of knowing something also means effecting certain changes in the environment with which the human organism is continuous. If the change is for the better—that is, if it carries out the purpose for which the "inquiry" was launched—the knowledge acquired is "true" in the only sense in which the achievement of truth is possible.

The only test for truth in an idea, therefore, is in its consequences in the life activities to which it leads. The only way of intelligently testing and controlling those consequences is through the method of experimental science. If the consequences of a proposition are good, the idea may have "warranted assertability." Of course the problem "what is good?" is a serious one in this as in every philosophy; Mr. Dewey deals with it at length in his ethical works. In general he considers it in relation to social ends.

Truth, or warranted assertability, is always relative, because the consequences of an idea may change with time or place. This necessarily follows from the doctrine that thinking or knowing always means involvement of the organism with the environment. Since the environment—natural, social, technological—is in constant change, the consequences of any activity involved with it are subject to change.

The search for knowledge must be continuous and arduous, but it is not, as in most older systems of philosophy, an aspiration toward any "ultimate reality" in the universe. It is a search for principles which will "work" here and now in a changing context; and there is no other way of getting them than through the experimental method. In the physical and natural sciences, all discoverable facts about a problem are collected, and explanations of them are tested by experiment. The simplest explanation which will account for all of them is set up as a "hypothesis," avowedly tentative and subject to change if new data should render it inadequate. The hypothesis is "true" to the extent that its consequences are favorable for furthering the investigation. That, according to Dewey, is the only kind of knowledge we can have about anything.

Many scientists who follow the scientific method within their specialties do not carry it through to their general view of the universe. Deweyites are critical not only of scientists who "go religious" outside their laboratories, but even of mathematicians and theoretical physicists who seek to fit the "gross facts" of observation to mathematically derived abstractions, instead of proceeding in the contrary direction.

Dewey is not a "materialist" if that word means one who believes in the finality of any alleged truth. The philosophy of the man who believes he has hold of absolute truth in the statement that "there is no reality except matter" is not more acceptable to Dewey than that of the man who says that "there is a personal God." But since Dewey does not readily concede "warranted assertability" to any proposition not in some way verifiable by the scientific method, he excludes supernaturalism as practically as did the old-fashioned dogmatic materialist.

III

There is no mind or "soul" in the traditional sense. This, if anything, is the key doctrine of Deweyism. Most previous philosophy, Dewey believes, has been infected by a double error of the Greeks: that there is some perfect or "ultimate" reality in the universe, and that it is discoverable by the use of a special intellectual faculty. Dewey finds no evidence in man of a non-material faculty which thinks, or which can be filled up with knowledge like a tank or a sponge. Nor is there a soul which is immortal or otherwise distinguishable from the body. Man is an organism engaged in an instinctive effort to adapt itself to the environment. There are many difficulties, many problems to be solved in this effort. Thinking, in Dewey's meaning of "inquiry," is one kind of effort to solve these problems, as walking is another. Intelligence grows in action and seeks to go beyond adaptation to control of the environment.

Mental activity like physical activity (the distinction is merely verbal) proceeds through habits developed by the organism in its relations with the environment. There is no life in the organism apart from such interaction. You cannot breathe without air, walk without a surface, talk without sound waves, or see without looking at something. Nor can you think without a similar interaction of your organism with things external to it, though these may be transferred to and distorted in the imagination. Thinking is like seeing. Sight is not something "in" the body; it is an *event* which occurs when the body is involved in a certain way with something else. In the same way, mind is not "in me." Mind is not a separate something which acts upon objects of thought. Like sight, mind is an *activity* which occurs when the organism interacts with the environment in a certain way. In Dewey's phrase, "mind is primarily a verb."

Mr. Dewey's view of the mind is critically important in his educational theories. The process of learning, for him, is not the accumulation of a mental stock of information. It is the acquisition by the organism of certain habits. Children are not born with minds. They acquire habits, including those of thought, which are not different in mode of origin from other habits. But their relations with the environment would be unbearably rigid and survival would be difficult if all activity had to be that of habit. Living is possible because habits are subject to modification; they are made flexible by impulses. The relation of impulse to habit varies greatly among individuals; it is a key to character and the proper concern of education.

Since there is no mind or thought apart from environmental interaction, it follows that there is no such thing as a soul or even a "self" which can exist (and be educated) apart from its own experiences. Man is continuous with the rest of nature, including the rest of mankind. The problem of environmental adjustment is so largely a social problem that the development of desirable social habits and the release of socially useful impulses are a most important responsibility of educators.

Man's efforts toward environmental adaptation include the development of mental and "spiritual" habits —that is, ideas or beliefs. These are not essentially different from the physical adaptations of the organism. There is nothing absolute or perfect or final about any of them. Some of them are better and some are worse for our purposes in our struggle for adaptation to and control of the environment.

There are no fixed moral laws. This follows from the foregoing. For centuries, Dewey believes, men wasted energy and confused themselves by efforts to find in religion or philosophy a set of immutable moral truths to which human nature should be made to conform. In most of the older religious traditions human nature was viewed with suspicion and subjected to efforts to make it behave properly in relation to some transcendental ideal. Dewey insists that human nature itself is the only source of workable moral guides. He believes that the effort to find transcendental moral rules has been doubly wrong—wrong in fact, because there is no known deity or "higher" reality whence such principles may be derived; and wrong in effect, because the effort to enforce that kind of moral law has separated the sphere of our present morality from the most important human activities in politics, economics, and other social relationships.

The wisdom or unwisdom of a moral rule, according to Dewey, depends upon its consequences in the activities it creates. The scientific method is the only proper procedure for establishing moral codes, as it is for obtaining any kind of knowledge. All the relevant data of individual and social psychology, of sociology, economics, and technology, as well as the natural sciences, must be applied to the problems of human behavior. We must, indeed, have principles and we must develop habits of conformity to them. But principles can never be absolute or final; they should be

bench marks of our progress in scientific morality.
They are subject to change, with due caution, for
thoroughly investigated reasons. Both the principles
themselves and the aptitude for changing them when
necessary should be properly related to our twin en-
gines of habit and impulse.

There is nothing "lax" about Dewey's proposed
morality of human nature. He was a rather austere
person in his own life, and he expected a high standard
of behavior in others. He also wanted to preserve
what he regarded as the real values in traditional religious sentiment. His famous work *A Common Faith*
is a plea for the release of those values from their involvement in what he regards as ancient superstitions
and reactionary religious institutions, that they may
be of modern service in a kind of noninstitutional
religion of humanity.

Human happiness is the consistent aim of Dewey's
moral theory, as he does not believe there is any future
existence in which the sorrows and inequities of this
life may be redressed. But he is scornful of ethical
short cuts and oversimplifications, such as the illusory
emancipation of the "Bohemian" who would seek
freedom from convention through slavery to passion.
He believes that the present maldistribution of happiness and suffering can be alleviated by educational
strengthening of habits of coöperation and generosity,
and the liberation of impulses to the same ends. Our
present faulty social habits are fixed in inequitable
institutions of government and property and the like.
Better habits will make better institutions, not vice
versa.

IV

Democracy is a moral value. Mr. Dewey was the
acknowledged philosopher of democracy as well as

of science, but his definition goes beyond the limited political meaning. It derives from the assumption of the worth of each human being, but this is not for him a truth dependent upon a unique creation or a supernatural destiny of man. Nor can Dewey accept the older philosophical idea of "natural rights" to the extent that it was dependent upon a notion of immutable natural law. His assertion of human value is validated by the consequences which flow from it in action.

Democracy is a moral value because it is the social order which encourages each individual to make the most effective use of his powers for living with maximum satisfaction; or in the scientific view, to achieve the most successful relationship of the organism to its environment. Since the environment is so largely social, this adjustment cannot be achieved for individuals without social effort—that is, without the development of strong habits of coöperation.

Most persons, including irreconcilable critics of pragmatism, will concede that the pragmatic case for democracy is a strong one. Anyone can see that the consequences of freedom will be desirable for himself, and no philosophical profundity is required for the further seeing that he will be most secure in the enjoyment of freedom under a social system which assures it for the other fellow.

In practice Dewey's attitudes put him definitely to the left of center, particularly in his suspicion of big business and in his willingness to see economic inequities reduced by political action. This willingness, however, is conditioned by the Deweyan view that there can be no comprehensive institutional change without a change of habits through education.

Dewey is *not* a Marxist. His philosophy is quite inconsistent with the "dialectic" of Marxian theory. Nor can Dewey, with his views of human nature and

conduct, share the Marxian expectation of extensive
social change primarily through political or revolutionary action. For many readers of Dewey, the transfer
of the Russian people by revolution from one tyranny
to another is striking confirmation of the accuracy of
his analysis of the social psychology of habit.

Dewey had no truck with Communism. His philosophy is so definitely hostile to the Marxian orthodoxy
of Lenin and Stalin that the efforts of an occasional
reactionary pamphleteer to link him with Communism
are the work of malice or ignorance. Dewey was opposed to the Soviet enterprise because he is philo-
sophically opposed to all absolutes, and most vehemently
to those which furnish pretexts for the curbing of
freedom. His views are clearly on record, and more:
the Communists devoted to him their bitterest invec-
tive when he undertook in 1937 the leadership of an
enterprise devoted to exposing the Stalinist frame-up
of Trotsky.

But, despite this anti-Communism, there is no aid
or comfort in Deweyism for the believer in free
economic enterprise. The only revolution which
Dewey endorses is that which will operate through
educational change of habits and impulses, but the
kind of society toward which he wants this change
to operate is definitely a species of socialism, different
as it may be from that of Marxian orthodoxy. Deweyism is no more acceptable to one who believes in economic liberalism than to one who believes in supernaturalism.

                                 v

Pragmatism justifies Progressive Education.   Dewey's
basic philosophical assumptions are more than well
hinged to his educational doctrines. For example, his
rejection of the traditional distinction of mind and

body is an indispensable assumption. I believe this
should be held in mind by parents who are assured
by Educationists that progressivist methods can stand
alone, on psychological justification, without reference
to Deweyan pragmatism. That assertion merely in-
vites a question about the kind of psychology used by
the Educationist.

Progressivism is logically consistent with instrumentalist philosophy right down the line. If there are
no absolutes in the history of ideas, it is of course
quite sensible to throw out of our schools much of the
lore of the past. If the "warranted assertability" of
any idea depends upon the environmental context,
which is constantly changing, there are few ideas of
the distant past which retain that title today, if they
ever had it. If human behavior depends upon patterns
of habit and impulse, as Dewey believes, instruction by
exhortation is largely useless. A school program related
to the view of man as a monistic biological organism
should involve the student in lively activities around
the solution of problems of living which most clearly
beset him. And if habits alone are not enough (since
rigidity of habit explains many present social ills),
the program should also provide for the liberation of
impulses useful for making habits flexible.

The Deweyan educational reform proposes to man-
age intelligently an educational process which—if
Dewey is right—operates inevitably whether we heed
it or not. He believes that moral and other instruction
of the hortatory type has never been really effective,
that we have *always* been educated through habit
formation. In Dewey's view, the habits most of us have
now were forced upon us during infancy and childhood when we were physically dependent upon adults.
They are our elders' habits. Habits have changed from
one generation to another, thanks to the changing environment and the modification of habit by impulse.

But the older process of change was haphazard and irrational. According to Dewey, it left unshaken too many habits which perpetuate social inequities. Or very occasionally, it shook them too violently in those upheavals called revolutions. Intelligent management of the habit and impulse patterns in youth is the rationale of progressive education. It explains those classroom practices (at their best) with which most parents are familiar, including those practices which have provoked caricature.

Viewing Dewey's educational theories in philosophical perspective disposes of many superficial arguments about the New Education. Take the argument about whether Latin is "good" for youngsters. If there are any ethical or esthetic absolutes in human experience, the stately moral exhortations of Cicero and the poetic beauty of Vergil certainly bring us close to the best of them. But if there are not, the preachments of an ancient Roman may be a waste of time. And reading Vergil may consume energy better used in developing habits of esthetic appreciation (for example, in interior decorating) more directly related to problems of suburban living today. If there is little use in reading those authors, there is no use for any but future specialists in the laborious learning of Latin. But the main argument depends upon the preliminary ifs.

What is the practical effect of Deweyism on the curriculum? Well, here is an evidence of its effect in its most extreme form. The following is a statement by an enthusiastic disciple of Dewey, Samuel Tenenbaum, the biographer of William Heard Kilpatrick, who spent a long lifetime indoctrinating prospective teachers with Deweyism:—

"The writer has seen a class of six hundred and more graduate students in education, comprising teachers, principals, superintendents, vote their opinion in overwhelming numbers that Greek, Latin and mathematics offered the least likely possibilities for educational growth; and with almost the same unanimity they placed *dancing, dramatics* and *doll playing* high on the list in this regard." (Italics mine.)

Admittedly this is extreme, but it is the logical end point of the New or Deweyan Education. A curriculum which has been heavily Deweyized is one which is built around the "real needs" or "felt needs" of the pupils. However, any definition of human "needs" necessarily involves some philosophical assumption about the nature of man, of society, of the universe. The argument of Progressive Education *versus* Traditional Education does not turn on the merits of doll playing *versus* Latin grammar. It turns on the question: Are there any "constants" in human thought? Are there any absolutes in ethics? Are there any immutable principles of anything?

Agreement with the basic philosophy of Mr. Dewey is the logical price of agreement with his educational theories. The progressive school enthusiast who wants the second without the first is entitled to like what he likes and to be as illogical as he chooses, but his enthusiasm may be no more than an eagerness to be in fashion.

You may happily agree with all of Mr. Dewey's basic ideas. But how many parents in your town would join in your agreement if they understood them? would you say 51 per cent? I should say about 5 per cent or less in my town. You may have no objection to a "shift," as Bode puts it, "from a morality of *cosmic* sanction to a morality of *social* sanction, from morality with a fixed content to morality which varies with conditions and circumstances as determined by empirical investigation. . . ." (Italics in the original.) But

how many members of your P.T.A. would join in
your acceptance of this ethical doctrine if they understood it? Not many. Most people in my town and
yours really believe that their ethical intuitions have
some cosmic anchor. And of course a great many
teachers, probably most of them, believe the same.
That may be reassuring for those parents who do not
find Mr. Dewey an acceptable mentor for their children's schools. But it is a reassurance which depends
precariously upon the kind of teacher who does not
really know what he is doing.

Despite Dewey's own unquestioned intellectual
stature and integrity, his educational doctrines have
opened in our schools a door wide enough to admit a
legion of pedagogical boondogglers. Precisely because
Progressive Education dispenses so far with tradition
and stakes so much upon the educational creativity
of the teacher, it is a method which would require
someone like a Dewey in every classroom for intelligent execution. In actuality, by the testimony of their
own rapid utterances, the typical graduates in Education today are the least fitted group in the community
to assume the responsibility for re-creating its cultural
aspirations.

But there is also political quackery in the new
pedagogy. In their constant use of the word "democracy," the educational interpreters of Dewey are
evading the first and most fundamental implication
of the word: the will of the community. There is an
implication here and there in Dewey's writings which
becomes explicit and vociferous in the writings of
some of his disciples; that disagreement with his philosophy will usually be inspired by "social" motives.
Unquestionably the Deweyite can turn up evidences
of opposition based on nothing more than a conservative fear of change on the part of bishops and bankers
and the like who tremble for the institutions which

have served them. But Mr. Dewey's philosophy would
be much more widely opposed—if it were more widely
understood—for reasons more important than the
apprehensions of the chief beneficiaries of the status
quo.

Most people are suspicious of pragmatism, not because they fear its effect upon their interests, but
because they believe it to be flatly wrong. If their
reasons for thinking so are less profound than a
philosopher's, if they are based on rather simple loyalties which should now be outmoded, then let Mr.
Dewey's interpreters engage in a forthright effort to
enlighten the adults of my town and others on the
blessings of instrumentalism. And this author will join
in a Voltairian effort (apocryphal or not) to defend
to the death their right to do so. But it is not their
right, in the meantime, to slip into the school of the
community a philosophy of education which, if understood, would be rejected by the great majority of
the people to whom the schools belong. That is a
travesty of "democracy." Of course the will of the
majority has no meaning over against "truth," but
the sanction of fixed truth is the very one which the
pragmatist, by definition, cannot evoke.

I am opposed to the substantial teaching of religion
in the public schools because the American people
have so many gods that none could be served in public
education without slighting others. At the same time,
and for the same reason, I am opposed to a philosophy
of education which takes for granted the falsity of all
gods. A nonreligious curriculum may and should be
quite compatible with an attitude of sincere respect
for all religions. The philosophy of Professor Dewey is
categorically incompatible with such an attitude. Even
those who take satisfaction in the enormous influence
of John Dewey sometimes admit that his philosophy
has not been very clearly comprehended. If it had been,

there might have been some misgivings. You know your
neighbors. How many of them would vote for Deweyism if they understood the philosophical ballot?

RELEVANT READING

Dewey, John, "On Some Current Conceptions of the Term
    'Self,' " *Mind*, XV (January, 1890).
—— "The Bearings of Pragmatism upon Education." I. *Pro-
    gressive Journal of Education*, I (December, 1908); II.
    Ibid., I (January, 1909); III. *Ibid.*, I (February, 1909).
—— "The Instrumental Theory of Truth," in Joseph Ratner,
    ed., *The Philosophy of John Dewey*. New York: Henry
    Holt & Company, Inc., 1928.
—— *Theory of Valuation*. International Encyclopedia of
    Unified Science, Vol. II, Foundations of the Unity of
    Science, No. 4. Chicago: The University of Chicago
    Press, 1939.
—— "The Basic Values and Loyalties of Democracy." *Ameri-
    can Teacher*, XXV (May, 1941).
—— "How is Mind to Be Known?" *Journal of Philosophy*,
    XXXIX (January, 1942).
Lynd, Albert, *Quackery in the Public Schools*. Boston: Little,
    Brown & Company, 1953.
Naumburg, Margaret, "The Crux of Progressive Education."
    New Republic, LXIII (June, 1930).
Schwab, Joseph, "The 'Impossible' Role of the Teacher in
    Progressive Education." *School Review*, LXVII (Summer,
    1959).

In Prospect

After John Dewey, What?

Jerome S. Bruner

In 1897, at the age of thirty-eight, John Dewey published a stirring and prophetic work entitled "My Pedagogic Creed." Much of his later writing on education is foreshadowed in this document.

Five articles of faith are set forth. The first defines the educational process: "All education proceeds by the participation of the individual in the social consciousness of the race. This process begins unconsciously almost at birth, and is continually shaping the individual's powers, saturating his consciousness, forming his habits, training his ideas, and arousing his feelings and emotions." A second article of faith embodies Dewey's concept of the school: "Education being a social process, the school is simply that form of community life in which all those agencies are concentrated that will be most effective in bringing the child to share in the inherited resources of the race, and to use his own powers for social ends. Education, therefore, is a process of living and not a preparation for future living." In a third credo Dewey speaks of the subject matter of education: "The social life of the child is the basis of concentration or correlation in all his training or growth. The social life gives the unconscious unity and the background of all his efforts

This selection appeared originally in the *Saturday Review*, June, 1961. Professor Bruner is the Director of the Center for Cognitive Studies at Harvard University.

and all his attainments. . . . The true center . . . is not science, nor literature, nor history, nor geography, but the child's own social activities." A view of educational method gives form to Dewey's fourth faith: "The law for presenting and treating material is the law implicit in the child's own nature." For Dewey, the law was that of action: "The active side precedes the passive in the development of the child-nature. I believe that consciousness is essentially motor or impulsive; that conscious states tend to project themselves in action." And finally, Dewey's fifth thesis: "Education is the fundamental method of social progress and reform."

One reads the document today with mixed feelings. Its optimism is classically American in its rejection of the tragic view of life. It defines truth in the pragmatic spirit: truth as the fruit of inquiry into the consequences of action. It expresses a firm faith not only in the individual's capacity to grow but in society's capacity to shape man in its own best image. The final lines of the creed are these: "Every teacher should realize the dignity of his calling; that he is a social servant set apart for the maintenance of proper social order and the securing of the right social growth. In this way the teacher always is the prophet of the true God and the usherer in of the true kingdom of heaven."

Yet the very wholesomeness—the optimism, the pragmatism, the acceptance of man's harmonious continuity with society—leaves one uneasy. For in the two-thirds of a century between 1897 and today, there has been not only a profound change in our conception of nature, but also of society and the world of social institutions. Perhaps more important, we have lived through a revolution in our understanding of the nature of man, his intelligence, his capabilities, his passions, and the forms of his growth.

Dewey's thinking reflected the changes, though he was limited by the premises of his philosophical position. But between Dewey's first premises and our day, there bristles a series of revolutionary doctrines and cataclysmic events that change the very character of the inquiry. Two world wars, the dark episode of Hitler and genocide, the Russian Revolution, the relativistic revolution in physics and psychology, the Age of Energy with its new technology, the sardonic reign of skeptical philosophy—all of these have forced a reappraisal of the underlying premises in terms of which we construct a philosophy of education.

Let us, then, re-examine the premises, being guided by what we know today of the world and of the nature of human nature. But there is matter that is liable to some misinterpretation in an enterprise such as this, and we do well to clear it up at the outset. One writes against the background of one's day. Dewey was writing with an eye to the sterility and rigidity of school instruction in the 1890s—its failure to appreciate particularly the nature of the child. His emphasis upon the importance of direct experience and social action was an implied critique of the empty formalism of education that did little to relate learning to the child's world of experience. Dewey did mighty service in inspiring a correction. But an excess of virtue is vice. We, in our day, are reconsidering education against the background of such an excess. Misunderstanding often converted Dewey's ideas into sentimental practice that he deplored: "Next to deadness and dullness, formalism and routine," he wrote in his Creed, "our education is threatened by no greater evil than sentimentalism." The sentimental cult of "the class project," of "life adjustment" courses, of fearfulness in exposing the child to the startling sweep of man and nature lest it violate the comfortable domain of his direct experience, the cloying concept of "readiness"—these are conceptions about children often divorced from experiment on the educational process, justified in the name of Dewey. His was a noble yet tender view in his time. But what of our times? In what form shall we speak our beliefs?

Education seeks to develop the power and sensibility of mind. The task of education is twofold. On the one hand, the educational process transmits to the individual some part of the accumulation of knowledge, style, and values that constitute the culture of a people. In doing so, it shapes the impulses, the consciousness, and the way of life of the individual. But education must also seek to develop the processes of intelligence so that the individual is capable of going beyond the cultural ways of his social world, able to innovate, in however modest a way, so that he can create an interior culture of his own. For whatever the art, the science, the literature, the history, and the geography of a culture, each man must be his own artist, his own scientist, his own historian, his own navigator. No person is master of the whole culture; indeed, this is almost a defining characteristic of that form of social memory that we speak of as culture. Each man lives a fragment of it. To be whole, he must create his own version of the world, using that part of his cultural heritage that he has made his own through education.

In our time, the requirements of technology press heavily upon the freedom of the individual to create images of the world that are satisfying in the deepest sense. Our era has also witnessed the rise of ideologies that subordinate the individual to the defined aims of a society, a form of subordination that is without compassion for idiosyncrasy and that respects only the instrumental contribution of the individual to the progress of the society. At the same time, and in spite of ideologies, man's understanding of himself and of his world—both the natural and social world—has deepened to a degree that warrants calling our age an intellectually golden one. The challenge of the times ahead is to employ our deeper understanding not only to the enrichment of society but to the enrichment of the individual.

It is true, as Dewey said many years ago, that all education proceeds by the participation of the individual in the social consciousness of the race, but it is a truth with a double edge. For all education, good and bad alike, is of that order. We know now to what degree, to take but one example, the very language one speaks conditions and shapes the style and structure of thought and experience. Indeed, there is reason to believe that thought processes themselves are internalizations of social intercourse, an inner colloquy patterned by early external dialogues. It is this that makes education possible. But education, by giving shape and expression to our experience can also be the principal instrument for setting limits on the enterprise of mind. The guarantee against limits is the sense of alternatives. Education must, then, be not only a transmission of culture but also a provider of alternative views of the world and a strengthener of the will to explore them.

After a half-century of startling progress in the psychological sciences, we know that mental health is only a minimum condition for the growth of mind. The tragedy of mental illness is that it so preoccupies the person with the need to fend off realities with which he cannot cope that it leaves him without either the nerve or the zest to learn. But mental health is a minimum condition. The powers of mind grow with their exercise. Adjustment is too modest an ideal, if it is an ideal at all. Competence in the use of one's powers for the development of individually defined and socially relevant excellence is much more to the point. After a half-century of Freud, we know that the freeing of instinct and inclination is not an end in itself but a way station along the road to competence. What is most prophetic for us about Freud in this second half of the century is not his battle against the fetters of rigid moralism, but his formula: "Where there was id, let there be ego."

Education must begin, as Dewey concluded his first article of belief, "with a psychological insight into the child's capacities, interests, and habits," but a point of departure is not an itinerary. It is equally a mistake to sacrifice the adult to the child as to sacrifice the child to the adult. It is sentimentalism to assume that the teaching of life can always be fitted to the child's interests, just as it is empty formalism to force the child to parrot the formulas of adult society. Interests can be created and stimulated. In this sphere it is not far from the truth to say that supply creates demand, that the challenge of what is available creates response. One seeks to equip the child with deeper, more gripping, and subtler ways of knowing the world and himself.

The school is entry into the life of the mind. It is, to be sure, life itself and not merely a preparation for living. But it is a special form of living, one carefully devised for making the most of those plastic years that characterize the development of *homo sapiens* and distinguish our species from all others. School should provide not simply a continuity with the broader community or with everyday experience. It is the special community where one experiences discovery by the use of intelligence, where one leaps into new and unimagined realms of experience, experience that is discontinuous with what went before, as when one first understands what a poem is or what beauty and power and simplicity inheres in the idea of the conservation-of-energy theorems—that nothing is lost, only converted, and that measure is universally applicable. If there is one continuity to be singled out, it is to convert the autistic sense of the omnipotence of thought of the young child into that realistic confidence in the use of thought that characterizes the effective man.

In insisting upon the continuity of the school with the community on the one side and the family on the other, John Dewey overlooked the special function of education as an opener of new perspectives. If the school were merely a transition zone from the intimacy of the family to the life of the community, it would be a way of life easily enough arranged. It is interesting to examine the educational systems of primitive societies. It is almost universal that there comes a point, usually at puberty, where there is a sharp change in the life of the boy, marked by a *rite de passage* that has as its effect the establishment of a sharp boundary between childhood ways and the ways of the adolescent.

It would be romantic nonsense to pattern our practices upon those found in preliterate societies. I would only ask that we attend to one parallel: that education not confuse the child with the adult and recognize that the transition to adulthood involves an introduction to new realms of experience, the discovery and exploration of new mysteries, the gaining of new powers. This is the heady stuff of education and it is its own reward.

In the *shtetl* of Eastern Europe, the traditional Jewish ghetto, the wise scholar was a particularly important figure—the *talmud khokhem*. In his mien, his mode of conversation so rich in allusion, his form of poise, the wise man was the image not of a competent but, rather, of a beautiful person. Traditional Chinese society also had its image of the beautiful person, one who blended knowledge and sentiment and action in a beautiful way of life. The ideal of the gentleman served perhaps the same function in Europe of the seventeenth and eighteenth centuries. It is perhaps in this spirit that Alfred North Whitehead urged that education must involve an exposure to greatness if it is to make its mark. I would urge that the yeast of education is the idea of excellence, and the idea of excellence comprises as many forms as there are individuals, each of whom develops his own image of excellence. The school must have as one of its principal functions the nurturing of images of excellence.

A detached conception of idealized excellence is not enough. A doctrine of excellence, to be effective, must be translatable into the individual lives of those who encounter it. What is compelling about the *talmud khokhem*, the Chinese scholar-administrator, the eighteenth-century gentleman, is that they embody ways of life to which each can aspire in his own way and from which each can borrow in his own style. I believe, then, that the school must also contain men and women who, in their own way, seek and embody excellence. This does not mean that we shall have to staff our schools with men and women of great genius, but that the teacher must embody in his or her own approach to learning a pursuit of excellence. And, indeed, with the technical resources opened by television and the like, one can also present the student and his teacher with the working version of excellence in its highest sense. In the years ahead, we shall learn that the great scholar, scientist, or artist can speak as easily and honestly to the beginner as to the graduate student.

The issue of subject matter in education can only be

resolved by reference to one's view of the nature of knowledge. Knowledge is a model we construct to give meaning and structure to regularities in experience. The organizing ideas of any body of knowledge are inventions for rendering experience economical and connected. We invent concepts such as force in physics, the bond in chemistry, motives in psychology, style in literature, as means to the end of comprehension. The history of culture is the history of the development of greater organizing ideas, ideas that inevitably stem from deeper values and points of view about man and nature. The power of great organizing concepts is not only that they permit us to understand and sometimes to predict or change the world in which we live; it lies also in the fact that ideas provide instruments for experience. Having grown up in a culture dominated now by the ideas of Newton with a conception of time flowing equably, we experience time moving with an inexorable and steady one-way arrow. Indeed, we know now, after a quarter of a century of research on perception, that experience is not had direct and neat, but filtered through the programed readiness of our senses. The program is constructed of our expectations and these are derived from our models or ideas about what exists and what follows what.

From this, two convictions follow. The first is that the structure of knowledge—its connectedness and the derivations that make one idea follow from another—is the proper emphasis in education. For it is structure, the great conceptual inventions that bring order to the congeries of disconnected observation, that gives meaning to what we may learn, and makes possible the opening up of new realms of experience.

The second conviction is that the unity of knowledge is to be found within knowledge itself, if the knowledge is worth mastering. To attempt a justification of subject matter, as Dewey did, in terms of its relation to the child's social activities is to misunderstand what knowledge is and how it may be mastered. The significance of the concept of commutativity in mathematics does not derive from the social insight that two houses with fourteen people in each is not the same as fourteen houses with two people in each. Rather, it inheres in the power of the idea to generate a way of thinking about number that is lithe and beautiful and immensely generative—an idea at least as powerful as, say, the future conditional tense in formal grammar. Without the idea of commutativity, algebra would be impossible. If set theory—now often the introductory section in newer curricula in mathematics—had to be justified in terms of its relation to immediate experience and social life, it would not be worth teaching. Yet set theory lays a foundation for the understanding of order and number that could never be achieved with the social arithmetic of interest rates and bales of hay at so much per bale. Mathematics, like any other subject, must begin with experience, but progress toward abstraction requires precisely that there be a weaning away from the obviousness of superficial experience.

There is one consideration of economy that is paramount. One cannot "cover" any subject in full—not even in a lifetime, if coverage means visiting all the facts and events and morsels. Subject matter presented so as to emphasize its structure will perforce be of that generative kind that permits reconstruction of the details or, at very least, prepares a place where the details, when encountered, can be fitted.

What, then, of subject matter in the conventional sense? The answer to the question "What shall be taught?" turns out to be the answer one gets to the question "What is nontrivial?" If one can once answer the question "What is worth knowing about?" then it is not difficult to distinguish between what about it is worth teaching and learning and what is not. Surely, knowledge of the natural world, knowledge of the human condition, knowledge of the nature and dynamics of society, knowledge of the past so that one may use it in experiencing the present and aspiring to the future—all of these, it would seem reasonable to suppose, are essential to an educated man. To these must be added another—knowledge of the products of our artistic heritage that mark the history of our esthetic wonder and delight.

A problem immediately arises concerning the symbolism in terms of which knowledge is understood and talked about.

There is language in its natural sense and language in its mathematical sense. I cannot imagine an educated man a century from now who will not be somewhat bilingual in this special sense—concise and adept in a natural language and mathematics. For these are the tools essential to the unlocking of new experience and the gaining of new powers. As such, they must have a central place in any curriculum.

Finally, it is as true today as it was when Dewey wrote that one cannot foresee the world in which the child we educate will live. Informed powers of mind and a sense of potency about coping are then the only instruments we can give the child that will be invariant across the transformations of time and circumstance. The succession of studies that we give the child in the ideal school need not be fixed in any but one way: whatever is introduced, let it be pursued continuously enough to give the student a sense of the power of mind that comes from a deepening of understanding. It is this, rather than any form of coverage over time, that matters most.

The process and the goal of education are one and the same thing. The goal of education is disciplined understanding. That is the process as well.

Let us recognize first that the opposite of understanding is not ignorance or simply "not knowing." To understand something is, first, to give up some other way of conceiving of it. Between one way of conceiving and a better way, there often lies confusion. It is one of our biological inheritances that confusion produces emergency anxiety, and with anxiety there come the defensive measures—flight, fright, or freezing—that are antithetical to the free and zestful use of mind. The limiting fact of mental life in child and adult alike is that there is a limited capacity for processing information—our span, as it is called, can encompass six or seven unrelated items simultaneously. Go beyond that and there is overload, confusion, forgetting. The degree to which material to be learned is put into structures by the learner will determine whether he is working with gold or dross. For this reason, as well as for reasons already stated, it is essential that before being exposed to a wide range of material on a topic, the child first have a general idea of how and where things fit. It is often the case that the development of the general idea comes from a first round of experience with concrete embodiments of an idea that are close to the child's life. The cycle of learning begins, then, with the particular and immediate, moves toward abstraction, and comes to a temporary goal when the abstraction can then be used in grasping new particulars in the deeper way that abstraction permits.

Insofar as possible, a method of instruction should have the objective of leading the child to discover for himself. Telling children and then testing them on what they have been told inevitably has the effect of producing bench-bound learners whose motivation for learning is likely to be extrinsic to the task at hand— pleasing the teacher, getting into college, artificially maintaining self-esteem. The virtues of encouraging discovery are of two kinds. In the first place, the child will make what he learns his own, will fit his discovery into the interior world of culture that he creates for himself. Equally important, discovery and the sense of confidence it provides are the proper rewards for learning. They are rewards that, moreover, strengthen the very process that is at the heart of education—disciplined inquiry.

The child must be encouraged to get the full benefit from what he learns. This is not to say that he should be required to put it to immediate use in his daily life, though so much the better if he has the happy opportunity to do so. Rather, it is a way of honoring the connectedness of knowledge. Two facts and a relation joining them are and should be an invitation to generalize, to extrapolate, to make a tentative intuitive leap, indeed even to build a tentative theory. The leap from mere learning to using what one has learned in thinking is an essential step in the use of mind. Indeed, plausible guessing, the use of the heuristic hunch, the best employment of necessarily insufficient evidence— these are activities in which the child needs practice and guidance. They are among the great antidotes to passivity.

Most important of all, the educational process must be free of intellectual dishonesty and those forms of cheating that explain without providing understanding. I have expressed the conviction elsewhere than any subject can be taught to anybody at any age in some form that is honest. It is not honest to present a fifth-

grade social studies class with an image of Christopher
Columbus as a typical American teen-ager musing
after school with his brother, Bart, about what lies
across the seas—even if the image set forth does happen
to mesh with the child's immediate sense of social experience. A lie is still a lie—even if it sounds like
familiar truth. Nor is it honest to present a sixth-grade
science class with a garbled but concrete picture of
the atom that is, in its way, as sweeteningly false as
the suburban image of Columbus given them the year
before. A dishonest image can only discourage the
self-generating intellectual inquiry out of which real
understanding grows.

I believe that education is the fundamental method
of social change. Even revolutions are no better than
the ideas they embody and the invented means for
their application.

Change is swifter in our times than ever before in
human history and news of it is almost instantaneous.
If we are to be serious in the belief that school must
be life itself and not merely preparation for life, then
school must reflect the changes through which we are
living.

The first implication of this belief is that means must
be found to feed back into our schools the ever deepening insights that are developed on the frontiers of
knowledge. This is an obvious point in science and
mathematics, and continuing efforts are now being in-
stituted to assure that new, more powerful, and often
simpler ways of understanding find their way back
into the classrooms of our primary and secondary
schools. But it is equally important to have this constant refreshment in fields other than the sciences—
where the frontiers of knowledge are not always the
universities and the research laboratories but political
and social life, the arts, literary endeavor, and the

rapidly changing business and industrial community. Everywhere there is change and with change, we are learning.

I see the need for a new type of institution, a new conception in curriculum. What we have not had and what we are beginning to recognize as needed is something that is perhaps best called an "institute for curriculum studies"—not one of them, but many. Let it be the place where scholars, scientists, men of affairs, artists, come together with talented teachers constantly to revise and refresh our curricula. It is an activity that transcends the limits of any of our particular university faculties—be they faculties of education, of arts and science, of medicine or engineering. We have been negligent in coming to a sense of the quickening change of life in our time and its implications for the educational process. We have not shared with our teachers the benefits of new discovery, new insight, new artistic triumph. Not only have we operated with the notion of the self-contained classroom, but also with the idea of the self-contained school—and even the self-contained educational system.

Let me consider again what I said about the images of excellence and the role of constant curricular refreshment in helping produce those images. The Nobel laureate or the Ambassador to the United Nations, the brilliant cellist or the perceptive playwright, the historian making use of the past, or the sociologist seeking a pattern in the present—these are men who, like the student, are seeking understanding and mastery of new problems. They represent excellence at the frontiers of endeavor. If a sense of progress and change toward greater excellence is to illuminate our schools, there must be a constant flowing back of their wisdom and effort to enliven and inform teacher and student

alike. There is not a difference in kind between the
man at the frontier and the young student at his own
frontier, each attempting to understand.

How put the matter in summary? Perhaps it is best to
parallel John Dewey's "Credo": That education is not
only the transmission of culture, but that it also gives
shape to the power and sensibility of mind so that
each person may learn how to inquire for himself and
build an interior culture of his own. That the school is
entry into the life of mind, with all this implies about
confidence in the use of mind to push to the limit and
test the implications of what each has come to know.
That the subject matter of education is knowledge
about the world and its connectedness, knowledge
that has a structure and a history that permits us to
find order and predictability in experience and delight
in surprise. That the method of education is the
method involved in any understanding—a disciplined
and responsible effort to know on one's own and to
convert what one has understood into an ordered rep-
resentation of the world that respects the particular
but recognizes the intellectual indispensability of the
abstract. That the school continues to be the principal
instrument of social progress in an era of swift change
and that, as such, it find means of constantly refresh-
ing and altering its instruction by feeding back the new
insights of our times into its curriculum. All of these
things depend in the end upon cultivating and giving
expression to the forms of excellence that emerge in
our varied society. Any aims less ambitious than these
are surely unworthy of the challenges we face.

RELEVANT READING

Bruner, J. S., *The Process of Education.* New York: Random House, Inc., 1963.

———, Goodnow, J. J., and Austin, G. A., *A Study of Thinking.* New York: John Wiley & Sons, Inc., 1956.

Dewey, John, *My Pedagogic Creed.* New York: E. L. Kellogg and Company, 1897.

INDEX